M000282076

The Jewish Art of Self Discovery

THE
JEWISH

ART

OF
SELF
DISCOVERY

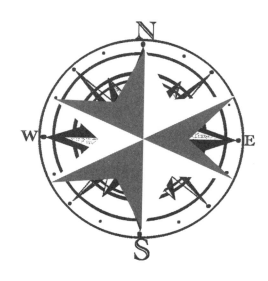

Benjamin Rapaport

The Jewish Art of Self Discovery
by Benjamin Rapaport

Copyright © 2013 by Benjamin Rapaport

All rights reserved. No part of this book may be used or reproduced in any manner whatsoever without written permission from the copyright owner, except in the case of brief quotations embodied in reviews and articles.

Typeset by Ariel Walden

Printed in Israel

First Edition
ISBN 978-965-524-130-3

Urim Publications   Lambda Publishers, Inc.
P.O.Box 52287   527 Empire Blvd.
Jerusalem 91521 Israel   Brooklyn, NY 11225 U.S.A.
                           Tel: 718-972-5449
                           Fax: 718-972-6307

www.UrimPublications.com

Dedication

THIS publication is dedicated in loving memory of

Dr. FELIX T. RAPAPORT,

my father. Papa was a world-famous pioneer in the field

of organ transplantation, excelling as a scientist, surgeon

and educator. He was also a survivor of Nazi Europe,

fleeing as a child to Santo Domingo, and then moving

to the United States as a teenager. His life experiences

and unique qualities formed a powerful, yet immensely

human personality, who worked tirelessly to increase

quality of life for others, to great effect. May this work

bring him nachas.

— B.R.

*T*HIS publication is dedicated

in loving memory of

Dr. FELIX T. RAPAPORT *z"l*

לעילוי נשמת

ר׳ נתן ב״ר מרדכי הכהן רפאפורט ז״ל

נפטר י״ט ניסן תשס״א

ת.נ.צ.ב.ה

by

GERALD and MADELAINE GREENBERG

Toronto, Canada

בס״ד

~ הרב מרדכי פרידלאנדר ~

ראש הישיבת אור חדש טלז-סטון יצ״ו
ורב מכון משמרת סת״ם בירושלים עה״ק תבב״א

הן בא לפנינו תלמידי וידידי מאז ועכשיו, מחשובי תלמידי דישיבת מיר ירושלים, הרב בנימין
זאב הכהן רפאפורט שליט״א, והראה לי תכריכי כתבים שלו שמתכונן להוציא לאור בעה״ת
בימים הקרובים, נכתב בשפת אנגלית, ועברתי עליו לפי מיסת הפנאי ומצאתי שהיא מלא
וגדוש בעצות והדרכות כשרות, נכתב בעומק המחשבה, מעשה אורג מתורתן של חז״ל
הקדושים, ואחרונים, בעלי מחשבה ובעלי ההשקפה הטהורה.

אני רואה בספר זה תועלת גדולה הן לצעירים, הן למבוגרים, לת״ח ולתלמידיהן, ולכל מי
שרוצה לעבוד על עצמו ימצא בו את מבוקשתו בעהי״ת.

והנני מברך את ידידי שחפץ ה׳ יצליח בידו לברך על המגמר בקרוב, ושיזכה להיות ממזכי
הרבים כחפץ לבו הטוב וכעתירת ידידו,

מברכו מרדכי פרידלנדר

Translation:

My dear student and friend of many years, one of the esteemed scholars of the Mir Yeshiva of Jerusalem, Rabbi BENJAMIN RAPAPORT, has shared with me his writings, which he intends to publish in the near future. They are written in English, and I have reviewed them and found them to be filled with helpful insights and guidance, written with depth of thought – a work of craftsmanship from the teachings of our holy Sages, latter commentaries, masters of Jewish thought and those pure in perspective.

I see in this work great benefit to young and old, to Torah scholars and their students. Whoever desires to work on who they are will find what they desire, with HASHEM's help.

I bless my friend that the desire of HASHEM succeed through him, that he successfully complete this project, being among those who bring merit to the many, according to the desire of his heart and the wishes of his friend.

With blessing,
MORDECHAI FRIEDLANDER

טל. (02) 579-6199 .פקס (02) 534-4540

There can be no greater impediment to success, happiness and self-fulfilment than the failure to know oneself.

The Torah is the repository of true wisdom. Rabbi BENJAMIN RAPAPORT has masterfully extracted from the rich Torah literature many insightful teachings that can enable a person to come to a self-awareness. *The Jewish Art of Self-Discovery* is a major contribution to Torah-oriented psychology.

Rabbi ABRAHAM J. TWERSKI, MD

Every person is a world – indeed, a universe – and it can take a lifetime (if we are lucky!) to master the terrain. Truly knowing yourself – your strengths, weaknesses, the uniqueness and individuality of your personality, what makes you tick – is the first step in attaining spiritual enlightenment and growth. One can spend a lifetime doing mitzvot and studying Torah, and that is wonderful and virtuous; but without self-understanding, behaviors may easily degenerate into the superficial, and motivation is likely to falter. Without self-understanding, there can be no self-mastery. If, for example, I do not know what makes me angry or depressed, I do not have the tools to control my anger or depression. Without self-understanding, a person will never perceive the unique role the ALMIGHTY has carved out for him and will not have the resilience to face the vicissitudes of life with optimism, courage and hope.

Self-knowledge was the cornerstone of Rav YISRAEL SALANTER's Mussar movement, but for various reasons, it has fallen out of vogue in much of contemporary Jewish education. Rabbi BENJAMIN RAPAPORT thus deserves a hearty yasher koach in trying to restore this foundational wisdom to its rightful place. In a remarkable book, *The Jewish Art of Self-Discovery*, he attempts to guide the reader through a rich tapestry of Torah sources – Tanach, Talmud, Midrash, Chassidus, Mussar and Kabbala – in order to enable the discovery of the irreplaceable "you." The work is filled with beautiful, striking and practical insights, and contains numerous exercises and charts that can help the reader apply abstract principles to his or her real life.

I highly recommend this book, and hope and pray that many will be inspired to find the greatest of all treasures – the treasure that HASHEM put within them.

Rabbi YITZCHAK BREITOWITZ,
Senior lecturer, Ohr Somayach, Jerusalem,
Former Rabbi of the Woodside Synagogue in Silver Spring, Maryland,
and Associate Professor of Law at University of Maryland

Congregation Aish Kodesh
of Woodmere
351 Midwood Road
Woodmere, N. Y. 11598
516 - 569-2660

RABBI MOSHE WEINBERGER

קהילת אש קודש דוודמיר

הרב משה וויינבערגער
מרא דאתרא

ב"ה

[handwritten letter, transcribed in print below]

[Hebrew handwritten lines]

The more I read this remarkable sefer, the more convinced I am that its time has arrived. *The Jewish Art of Self Discovery* is a work of art. The artist is Reb BINYAMIN RAPAPORT, an individual I have known for many years. His ability to capture the essence of avodas HASHEM in such a clear and elegant way has given birth to a new masterpiece in the growing world of English Torah literature. Emunah (faith) is, in fact, an *umnus* – a skill, an art – that was programmed by the CREATOR into each and every one of us. The difficulty lies in uncovering, in discovering that burning fire of Emunah simmering within.

Reb Binyamin's sefer will be an invaluable tool in the hands and heart of any true seeker of Emunas Yisrael. The author is filled with ahavas haTorah and yiras shomayim as well as a longing to be *mechazek* (to strengthen) the many *mevakshei* (seekers of) HASHEM of our generation.

בצפי' לראות בהרמת קרן ישראל וגילוי נשמתה
(With yearning to see the uplifting of the pride of Israel and the revelation of its soul)

משה וויינברגר
(HaRav MOSHE WEINBERGER shlita)

Rabbi Yitzchak Berkovits
Sanhedria HaMurchevet 113/27
Jerusalem, Israel 97707
02-5813847

יצחק שמואל הלוי ברקוביץ
ראש רשת הכוללים לינת הצדק
סנהדרי׳ה המורחבת 113/27
ירושלם ת״ו

Bs"D Jerusalem 6 Av, 5772

So many of our brethren are searching. Having lived their lives by instinct and social conditioning, they seek more. Intuition insists on there being something deeper. Young Jews travel the globe in search of their inner selves. Ironically, the secret of spirituality lies in the volumes of our own ancient tradition.

Many practicing young Jews preoccupied with the technical aspects of TORAH also yearn for spirituality. They, too, are unaware of that dimension of the very TORAH they study.

My dear friend Rabbi BINYAMIN RAPAPORT has spent years combining intense study of HALACHA with the development of an understanding of his own inner self based on principles of TORAH. This work reflects the scholarship, depth and creativity that the author is all about.

It is my hope that many will find in it the inner self they have been seeking, and will proceed to embrace the totality of TORAH – its wisdom and warmth. May the author make use of his many talents to assist more and more of our brethren in pursuit of a relationship with The CREATOR.

Sincerely,

Harav YITZCHAK BERKOVITZ shlita

CONTENTS

Contents

Contents

AUTHOR'S NOTE

One of the most beautiful shuls in all of Cracow is the Synagoga Izaaka. Dating back to the 1600s, and having been badly damaged by the Nazis in the 1930s, today it is a historic site, frequented by tour groups, which houses photographs and documentary films. There is a famous Chassidic legend surrounding the building of this shul and its patron, Reb Isaak. I believe that this tale has become so well known because of the truth within all of us that it touches:

Isaac Yaklish was a poor Jew who lived in Cracow. Day by day he struggled to put bread on the table for his large family. One night he dreamt that if he would travel to Prague, next to the courtyard of the king, underneath a bridge, deep in the ground, he would find a great treasure. He told himself that it was only a dream. Even the thought of making such a journey for someone in his circumstances was laughable. Who knows if there was any treasure there at all?

But night after night, he kept having the same dream. He started to think, maybe there really is a treasure there. Maybe, if somehow I can get there, I will find a treasure and solve all my worries, once and for all.

He made up his mind that, come what may, he had to go. He borrowed money from whomever would lend it to him and managed to scrape together enough to travel in the barest of ways. Isaac set out for Prague.

After many days of hard traveling, often by foot, and even more often with a hungry stomach, he finally arrived in Prague. Isaac made his way to the king's palace. He was finally there.

He saw the palace just as he had dreamt it. The courtyard and the bridge next to it were exactly as he had envisioned. But there was one detail he had not foreseen.

As he approached the bridge, next to the courtyard of the king, he saw soldiers standing there keeping watch. He waited for nightfall, but the soldiers were there by night as well. He sadly realized that it would be impossible for him to dig under the bridge without being stopped.

Isaac felt like crying. He had come so far and endured so much just to get to Prague. How could he go home and face his family, returning more empty-handed than he had come. Isaac had never felt more stuck.

Not knowing what else to do, the next day he spent his time pacing back and forth alongside the bridge. He walked its length, lamenting his situation until night fell. When night fell, he returned to his lodgings to get what little rest he could. The next day as well, he returned to the bridge and continued his sad march alongside it. For several days, he kept this up.

The General of the Army noticed Isaac walking dejectedly next to the bridge, day after day. He was curious and called Isaac over to find out his story. The General began, "I have noticed you here for the last couple of days walking back and forth by this bridge. What are you looking for, or for whom are you waiting?"

Isaac, not knowing what else to do, decided to tell the General his story. Who knows, maybe the General would help? He told the General how, night after night, he had dreamt of a great treasure buried under the bridge. And that he had traveled all the way from Cracow to Prague in order to dig for it.

Upon hearing Isaac's story, the General burst out laughing. He said to Isaac, barely able to contain himself, "For the empty stuff of dreams you went to such trouble?! Who believes in such foolishness?!

I also had a dream. In my dream I was told that I should travel to Cracow. And there I should look for Isaac Yaklish. And if I will dig in his house, under his oven, I will find a fantastic treasure there. Do you think that for even a second, I would be so stupid as to believe in such dreams and travel all the way to Cracow?!"

When Isaac heard the words of the General, he knew why he had come. His real reason for coming to Prague was not to dig under the bridge. It was to hear from the General where his own treasure was to be found. Not next to the courtyard of the king, but in his own house, under his own oven.

He immediately traveled home, dug beneath his oven, and found a tremendous treasure there. In a moment, his fortune had changed. From these riches he built a magnificent shul,[1] which to this day is called by his name.

Life is about searching for treasure. It is about uncovering an inner wealth that we already possess. When we find our treasure, not only are our own lives enriched, but so too are the lives of many others. This work is intended as a companion for all those who seek their treasure.

1. Jewish house of worship

PREFACE

One of the oldest kabbalistic texts, the Sefer Yetzira,[1] teaches that the world was created with "sefer, sefer, and sippur," which means with a book, a book, and a story. There are many explanations of what this means, and I would like to share with you my own. The kabbalists teach that everything that happens to each of us is contained in the Torah. This is the first sefer, the "book" of each individual's life, from the perspective of the heavens looking down. The second "book" is how each one of us reads the first book, our take on life, which invariably has more to do with who we are than anything the first book actually says. And the "story" is what we tell others about the first two, the face we show to the world, and everything that is involved in that.

This book is my attempt to find wholeness between these three facets of life. It is an exploration of each of these dimensions; our relationship to the Torah and G-d, our relationship to who we are, and our relationship to others. My aspiration is that through these pages, the reader will develop a deeper understanding and connection in each of these relationships, and between them, and find greater wholeness in their lives.

In the journey of life and in writing this book, I have been blessed with gifted teachers, exceptional friends, and passionate students. Even more importantly, Hashem has blessed me with a loving and supportive family, most especially my wife, Michaella. Whatever wisdom may be on the pages of this book, I gratefully owe to them. And whatever mistakes you may find, you can credit to me, and please have the kindness to let me learn from you as well.

Wishing you success in everything,

Benjamin

1. *The Book of Creation*, attributed to the patriarch Abraham

ACKNOWLEDGMENTS

This book would have never been possible without the help of a number of extraordinary individuals. As the saying goes, it takes a village to raise a child. In my case, there have been quite a few villages and exceptional people who have blessed and enriched my life with their time, kindness, and wisdom.

Over the last twenty years, I have had the privilege of being involved either full-time, or almost full-time, in Torah study. This was only possible because of the deep belief my parents had in my potential and their willingness to support my dreams. This is all the more remarkable considering that I was raised with the mantra, "You can do whatever you like – after you get your MD." Whatever I may have achieved is touched by their generosity. May this book be a merit for the soul of my father, Dr. Felix T. Rapaport, of blessed memory, and for my mother, Mrs. Margaret Rapaport, Yibadel L'Chaim Tovim. Your love and dedication stand before my eyes always.

Over the last eleven years, I have enjoyed the blessing of becoming part of the Greenberg Family of Toronto and being welcomed in like a son by my wonderful in-laws, Gerald and Madeleine Greenberg. Who my family and I have become would never have been possible without you. Thank you for your love and tremendous generosity, including the sponsorship of this project in memory of my father. May Hashem bless you with much nachas from all your children l'netzach netzachim.

My initial entry into serious Torah study began at Neveh Zion in Israel. The warmth, dedication, and patience of the Rebbeim there provided a unique opportunity for me to come to love and appreciate Torah learning and those who live it. In my journey, I have found few better models of people who teach so well by example. My primary rebbe there, Rabbi Eliyahu Meir Klugman shlit"a, has been particularly instrumental in my development. Very early on, our relationship transcended learning and has evolved into a close familial bond continuing to grow for nearly two decades.

In the Mir Yeshiva, where I have spent twelve of my last twenty years, I had the great blessing of having enjoyed a close relationship with the Rosh Yeshiva, Rav Nosson Tzvi Finkel zt"l. It is impossible for anyone who did not know him to imagine how such an incredibly busy person, with significant health difficulties, could be so available to so many people. He loved his students with his entire heart, lifting us up to see ourselves through his eyes. May his remembrance be a blessing forever.

In Beis Medrash Gevoha of Lakewood, where I became a rabbi and a husband, there were three individuals in particular who showed me great kindness. The first was the Rosh Yeshiva, Rav Dovid Schustal shlit"a, who welcomed me with warmth from day one, and made the time to learn with me weekly Mishnas Rebbe Aharon. The second was Rabbi Yitzchok Koslowitz shlit"a, my rebbe and chavrusa for Taaruvos, who opened me up to the excitement and satisfaction of learning sugyos aliba d'hilchoso and paved the way for me to become a musmach of BMG. The third was Rabbi Yissachar Rothschild zt"l. Rabbi Rothschild was an exquisite soul, who introduced me to a Ramchal I never knew before. He was a mentor and a friend who would often share of his insight, caring, and breadth of being until the early hours of the morning, many Thursday nights. His presence is deeply missed by all who knew him.

I also want to thank Rav Mordechai Friedlander shlit"a, who, over the last twenty years, has been a significant role model in my life and has blessed me with astute advice and guidance, steering me away from bad decisions and helping me to make better ones at crucial crossroads.

Furthermore, I would like to express my appreciation and gratitude to Rabbi Abraham Twerski, MD, who has been an advisor, mentor, and role model since I met him nearly twenty years ago, and to thank him for reviewing this book and so generously commenting on it.

In addition, I would like to thank Dr. Yisrael Levitz of the Neve Family Institute, and the entire staff there for providing me with an incredible education and training as a psychotherapist. I would like to particularly thank several instructors and supervisors who deeply impacted and improved my understanding and practice of psychotherapy: Mrs. Rachel Ackerman, MSW, Mrs. Marci Jablinowitz, MSc., Mrs. Miriam Timsett, MSW, and Mr. David Levinstein, MSW.

In my academic career, I particularly benefited from the brilliance of Dr. Susan Jackson and her passion for excellence in theory as well as practice.

In my clinical development, I would also like to thank Nitai Melamed, MA, who opened me up in more ways than one and helped me to understand myself and others in a much deeper way.

I would also like to thank my clients for having shared themselves and their struggles with me. As much as anyone, you have taught me about myself and the challenges and joys of the journey of life. Over the last four years, during which time this book came to be, there have been a number of wonderful people who have been instrumental in its development:

My rebbe, Rabbi Yitzchok Berkovitz shlit"a, has provided immeasurable insight both in regards to the content and the form of this work. Who Rabbi Berkovitz is speaks more clearly and beautifully that any words could. I am deeply grateful for the opportunity to know him.

My former chavrusa, dear friend, and mentor, Henry Schachar, has edited countless pieces over the years, providing honest feedback and incisive suggestions for improvement. This work has benefited greatly from his acumen and generosity of heart.

My friend, Ben Ettun, has helped me to stay goal-focused and motivated, especially when I have gotten discouraged or distracted.

My students at Tzamah Nafshi have given me the gift of being able to test the ideas in this book in the laboratory of life. They have enriched me, and the material in this book, profoundly with their passion for truth and desire for growth.

My editor at Urim, Ms. Sara Rosenbaum, has significantly elevated the writing and clarity of this work with her astute and sensitive touch. I greatly appreciate the enthusiasm she felt for this work and the value she attributed to it, both of which inspired me to continually improve it, as did her insightful comments and corrections.

I would also like to thank Tzvi Mauer of Urim Publications for his interest in this work, his willingness to publish it, and the quality he and his team bring to bear upon the projects they undertake.

Acharon Acharon Chaviv, without the cooperation, encouragement, and patience of my remarkable eizer k'negdo, Michaella, this book would not exist. May Hashem bless her with nachas from me, and from our children, l'netzach netzachim.

And finally, last in deed and first in thought, is Hashem. I am deeply grateful and humbled for the unexpected path my journey has taken, and the myriad blessings and opportunities which have met me along the way, not least among them, being able to share of His wisdom with others. May it be His will that this work find favor in His eyes.

—Benjamin Rapaport
Jerusalem 5772

INTRODUCTION

"Educate a child according to their way."[1]

Rabbi Kalonymus Kalman Shapira, the Piasetzna Rebbe, burned with a passion to ignite and reveal the light within every Jewish soul. He was a master at recognizing and developing an individual's potential. In his diary he wrote:

> A person must individuate himself qualitatively from others. This goes beyond not being bound by the habits, customs, and opinions of others; thinking one's own thoughts. This is a given. Without this, a person is neither a Jew, nor a human being. Rather, a distinct and unique personality must be revealed from within.
>
> In learning Torah and serving G-d, it is not a question of amount, or how intelligent one is, but rather an issue of inner quality, which needs to be revealed; a personalized approach to learning and service, which rises forth from the depths of the individual. So much so, that when one hears a Torah thought or a spiritual practice, everyone can recognize that it issued forth from the mind of this thinker, from the heart of this servant of G-d. Take for example the works of Maimonides or Nachmanides. Each is distinct and identifiable as being their work, in the style of wisdom and personal expression revealed.
>
> Why is this so visible? Because their essence, their unique, individuated form, was brought forth and expressed in the Torah and wisdom they revealed.[2]

1. Mishlei, 22:6
2. *Tzav Veziruz*, 10

Possessing a unique light and bearing a responsibility to bring it out into the world is not limited to the likes of Maimonides and Nachmanides. Each of us was endowed with something special to express in the world. If not for this, we would not be here. Finding this treasure and sharing it with the world is what life is about.

INDIVIDUALITY

"Just as their faces are different, so are their minds."[1]

To recognize and develop our potential, we need to appreciate the individual, unique nature of our own minds. This understanding allows us to chart a course of personal development that is appropriate to who we are. Following someone else's path, even if it is a good one for them, will not necessarily take us where we need to go.

"One who goes in their straightness fears G-d."[2]

The Vilna Gaon explains:

> Each person possesses a nature, unique unto himself. Therefore, each person must walk the path that he needs. Also, every person has a specific weakness, different from their neighbor's, which he must guard himself against. At the same time, their neighbor has his own weakness, for which he needs his own safeguards.
>
> As a result, each person must travel their own path, even if in the eyes of others it seems like a bad one. Such a perception results because the needs of the person [being judged] are not known to the person judging them. If despite such disapproval, a person stays true to their path, he is the one who is G-d fearing.[3]

Disapproval can be derailing. It is human nature to desire the approval of others, and the fear of losing that approval can be daunting to the point that some people will unconsciously choose approval over being who they really are. This is a tragic loss.

1. *Mishneh Torah*, Hilchos Deos, 1:1; Also Rav Tzaddok HaKohen, *Pri Tzaddik*, Shemos, Parshas Shekalim for explanation. Also *Sfas Emes*, Bamidbar, Parshas Korach.
2. *Mishlei*, 14:2
3. *Peirush HaGRA on Mishlei*, 14:2

When this type of loss happens, it leaves a painful void within the approval seeker. But instead of trying to fill this void by gaining greater self awareness, approval seekers generally try to fill this hole with the approval and praise of others. This is like trying to quench thirst with salt water.

Perhaps, they think, that if they will do as others do, they will gain the approval or acceptance they feel is so important. And then they will be somebody. The sad thing is that they are already somebody, and that somebody is getting buried deeper and deeper the more they look outside themselves for significance.

In contrast, people who create personal safeguards to protect themselves from their shortcomings know who they are. Even when their fences are unappealing to others, this is much less important than being true to their inner core. They are driven by something much deeper than public opinion. They are driven by a truth which stems from the essence of their being.

Having the strength to listen to our own voice even when others disapprove is no small thing. It requires being connected to who we are and having the courage to live from a deeper place. In that place, our concern with G-d's approval far outweighs any concerns we have with the approval of others.[4]

Reflection

What are some personal safeguards which could help me?

_____

_____

What do I give up for the approval of others

_____

_____

What would I do if I cared less about approval?

_____

_____

4. *Chovos Halevavos*, Shaar Ahavas Hashem, chap. 6

STRENGTHS

As important as it is to recognize our weak points and develop appropriate safeguards, it is even more essential to recognize our strengths, and know how to develop them. Our strengths are the tools we have been given to make our mark in the world. As Rabbi Yerucham Levovitz, the remarkable educator of the Mir Yeshiva[1] expressed, "Woe unto he who does not know his weaknesses. But woe and woe unto he who does not know his strengths, for even the tools which he possesses to elevate himself with, he does not know."

The Midrash in *Yalkut Shimoni* metaphorically conveys the beauty of recognizing and utilizing one's strengths:

> There are those who are beautiful to their garments, yet their garments are not beautiful unto them. There is a wealthy man, yet his name is not according to his wealth. There is a poor man, yet his name is not according to his poverty. There is a strong man, yet his name is not according to his might. There is a weak man, yet his name is not according to his weakness . . . Job was unlike these. Rather, charity to others was beautiful to Job, and Job was beautiful regarding charity to others. "I cloaked myself in charity – and I was cloaked by it."[2]

The Midrash articulates how Job possessed the strength of charity and beautifully expressed it in his life. At the same time, not everyone utilizes their strengths so superbly. As a result, it is possible to have a wealthy

1. Academy for the study of Talmud
2. *Yalkut Shimoni*, Iyov, Remez 917

person whose name[3] is not related to their wealth, because they did not use it to help others. Similarly, there can be a strong person whose name is not related to his strength because he did not use his strength to make a difference in the world. In contrast, there are those who despite being in a situation of lacking transcend the challenges of their circumstances. "There is a poor man, yet his name is not according to his poverty ... there is a weak man, yet his name is not according to his weakness."

Being a success in life is a combination of not succumbing to our weaknesses, while at the same time realizing our strengths. It can be challenging, though, to recognize and value our own strengths. We see others around us who seem to be successful in one way or another and it is easy to think that it is their strengths which are worthwhile and which we should emulate. Unfortunately, we often do this at the expense of appreciating our own strengths.

As tempting as it may be to imitate others, if we hope to enjoy our own success, we need to invest ourselves in the strengths that fit us. When we try to be someone we are not, it just does not fit, and sooner or later, something gives. As one great thinker expressed, "Don't walk around in borrowed clothing."

Historically, the Jewish people have been very particular about not pretending to be something we are not. We find a powerful example of this in the case of Eliezer Zeira, who stood in the marketplace dressed like a mourner. The officers of the Reish Galusa[4] asked him about his mode of dress. He answered them that he is in mourning over the destruction of Jerusalem. They questioned him, 'Are you such an elevated person that it is appropriate for you to mourn over Jerusalem?'[5] They thought he was putting on airs, and he was imprisoned, until it was clarified that he was a great Sage.

Through recognizing our signature strengths, and working to express them, we develop our unique potential. In doing so, we bring into the world the light that we were put here to reveal. What greater success could there be?

3. The Midrash uses the term "name" to convey that which a person reveals of himself in the world, like a name, which is what a person is known by to others.
4. Jewish political leader during the exile, following the destruction of the Holy Temple
5. *Bava Kama*, 59a

Reflection

What are some of my greatest strengths?

_____

_____

_____

_____

_____

What are some things I can do to develop these strengths?

_____

_____

_____

_____

AWARENESS

Knowing who we are, and are not, with clarity can be challenging. Our inner worlds are as vast as the outer world, encompassing a multitude of elements. Despite being so attached to ourselves, our knowledge of this inner world can be pretty limited.

Quite frankly, many of us do not want to know this inner world. Instead, we lead lives focused on the external, recoiling from looking within, even for a moment. It is as if we are afraid of being burnt by coming into contact with some strange and hidden place – our inner reality.[1] As long as we continue to do this, we will be unable to develop who we are.

How can we achieve the necessary awareness to see into this inner world and live in congruence with it, developing our inner greatness?

The Baal Shem Tov taught that everything we see around us is a mirror through which Providence shows us to ourselves. Life is bursting with meaning. Everything that happens to us, and around us, has a message. Living with this awareness, that our day-to-day life is an ongoing communication with G-d, lies at the heart of being inwardly awake.

Rebbe[2] Zusha, the famous tzaddik,[3] lived with this consciousness. One day, he was traveling along a road and was approached by a non-Jew whose wagon had fallen. The wagon was filled with hay, and the wagon owner asked Rebbe Zusha to help him lift it up. Rebbe Zusha replied that he was not able to. The man replied, "You can – but you just do not want to!"

---

1. *Alei Shur*, vol. 1, pt. 3
2. Honorary title for a leader of Chassidim
3. Person of exceptional piety

Rebbe Zusha understood that he was being given a message:

The lower "hei" (the last letter of G-d's four-letter name, which connotes His revealed presence in this world) had fallen. If he wanted to, he could lift it up (he could reveal the presence of G-d in the world). He just did not want to![4]

On a similar note, our Sages ask: Why is the section of the Torah discussing a Sotah (woman suspected of having had illicit relations) juxtaposed to the section discussing a Nazir[5] (one who has taken a temporary oath to abstain from wine)? Apparently, these are two unrelated concepts, so why does the Torah place them together?

The Sages answer that when a person sees another's demise they identify with the other's behavior on a certain level. They recognize the forces which brought the other person to stumble and sense those forces within themselves. As a result, they feel an inner need to put up a fence, so as not to fall down the same slippery slope.

The Nazir takes an oath to abstain from wine because he is afraid that if he drinks and lowers his inhibitions he may also stumble like the Sotah. He pays attention to what is going on inside himself, when he sees her fall, and takes preventive measures not to follow suit. Such a Nazir is living with self awareness.

Through paying attention to the events of our daily lives, and listening to their message, we can come to know ourselves better. Little by little we can cultivate a consciousness which connects us to who we are inside. This awareness enables us to develop who we are and live in a way which is true to ourselves.

Reflection

How much awareness do I bring to the events of my life?

_____

_____

_____

_____

4. *Pri Tzaddik*, Pesach (30)
5. *Sotah*, 2b

What are some messages that my life events have contained?

_____
_____
_____
_____

What could I do to live with more awareness?

_____
_____
_____
_____

WHOLENESS

What are the elements which compose us?

Man is a composite of body and spirit. The combination of these elements is so pervasive that every thought, word, and action represents a meshing of physical and spiritual parts. The partnership of these varied components is so integral to life that separating them is synonymous with death.

To be whole, inside and out, we need to achieve a working harmony between these different parts. Achieving personal wholeness is a balancing act in which both our physicality and spirituality are addressed, in accordance with where we are up to in our life journey. An overemphasis or neglect, of either body or soul, results in imbalance and fragmentation.[1]

When Hillel the Elder left the house of study, his students escorted him. They asked him, "Where are you going?" Hillel replied, "I am going to perform a kindness with the guest inside my house [and take care of his physical needs]."

They asked, "And every day you have a guest inside your home?" [This was a part of his daily schedule.]

Hillel answered, "And is my soul not a guest within the house of my body, that today it is here and tomorrow it is gone?"[2]

Hillel appreciated the nature of his body and soul and treated each accordingly. On his level of greatness, taking care of his physicality was only a means to sustaining his spirituality.[3] And at the same time, de-

1. *Kuzari*, Maamar Shlishi
2. *Vayikra Rabbah*, 34:3
3. *Be'er Mayim Chaim*, Toldos, chap. 26

spite his deep involvement in matters of the soul, he did not neglect what was needed to be physically well. To do otherwise would have been at the expense of wholeness.

To achieve the necessary balance, our Creator endowed us with a special gift called *daas*. Daas is like an inner compass, which alerts us to states of inner wholeness, or lack thereof. It is the faculty through which thought is bound to action, and intellect is merged with emotion.[4] It informs our choices of what to connect to and what to separate from.

When we follow the needle of our inner compass toward greater wholeness, we experience a heightened sense of inner balance. Both our body and our soul respond positively to being in harmony. When we glimpse the profound unity of being whole, it is the experience of connecting to a deep inner light, shining forth from a point in eternity.

In life, we need to follow the example of Hillel and give both our spirituality and physicality what they need to function optimally. Our body and our soul are at their best when the needs of each are met. And if the greatest Sage of his day needed to devote time, on a daily basis, to being in balance, all the more so do we.

Reflection

What is the balance between my body and soul like?

_____

_____

_____

When have I experienced a greater sense of wholeness?

_____

_____

_____

What are some things I can do to be more whole?

_____

_____

_____

4. *Alei Shur*, vol. 1, Sec. 3

REVELATION

Harmony between body and soul is expressed in the connection between our thoughts and our actions. Our faculty of thought has incredible spiritual potential, but if it is not joined to the physical world, it takes us nowhere. Only by joining spiritual thought to corporal action can we move upwards.

Rabbi Acha taught,

> One who learns in order to do merits divine revelation. What is the reason? For the verse states, "that you should watch to do all that is written, then your path will meet with success and you will understand ['understand' here is conveyed by the term 'maskil']" – and the term 'maskil' connotes Divine Revelation . . ."[1,2]

Also, Nachmanides wrote to his son in the famous "Letter of Nachmanides": "Each time you get up from your learning, reflect carefully to see what you can put into practice."

When we practically apply all that we learn to our lives, we are able to reach ever deeper levels of inner richness. An internal refinement transpires as we rise to the challenge of taking action in the face of adversity, from within and without. In walking this path, we can elevate ourselves to the level of being connected to the divine spirit and being able to experience revelation.

Elijah the prophet proclaimed the universality of this principle: "I testify by the heavens and earth, that any man or woman, Jew or non-

---

1. *Vayikra Rabbah*, Parsha 35
2. The root of the term "maskil" is "sechel," which is a term used to convey a refined level of soul perception.

Jew, slave or maidservant – according to a person's actions, the divine spirit will rest upon them."[3]

Our body and soul experience harmony when they work together for a higher purpose. This accord elevates both parts. The result is being able to access a superior level of spirituality where divine insight is possible.

Reflection

What are the benefits of translating spiritual thought into action?

_____

_____

_____

_____

What are some examples of how I have translated thought into action?

_____

_____

_____

_____

What have those experiences been like?

_____

_____

_____

_____

What can I do to apply what I learn more often?

_____

_____

_____

_____

3. *Eliyahu Rabbah*, Parsha 10

SELF-KNOWLEDGE AND TRANSCENDENCE

Our familiarity with our inner terrain makes it possible to traverse it. Without this, it is possible to go through life with the tranquility of the ignorant, stumbling where others may stumble, and doing acts of kindness as others may do, but not much else. Only by developing our self-knowledge can we aspire to something more.

Recognizing a few strengths and weaknesses falls short of really knowing who we are. Rather, when we are aware of the awesome heights we are capable of reaching, and at the same time, of the depths we can descend to, this is true self-knowledge. This knowing is elevating and humbling as one.

Deep self-awareness elevates us above desire and prejudice and brings us to identify with something more profound, more primary. This consciousness draws a line between our essential self and the varied forces which pull at us. To the extent that we hold onto this mindfulness, we remain connected to our real self.

In the ongoing inner struggle with varied pulls and pushes, there is an "I" which stands above all these. It is the quality of self that allows us to stand outside ourselves and look within. From this vantage point, we are able to identify ourselves as standing on a higher ground, above the spray of the storm which rages on the surface.

One of the greatest kindnesses we can do for ourselves is to make the time to connect to this "I" once in a while, and lift ourselves up. As Rabbi Menachem Mendel of Kotzk commented on the verse, "And a man shall not cheat his friend"[1] – a person needs to be his own friend and not

---

1. *Vayikra*, 25:17

cheat himself. In order to befriend ourselves, it is necessary to devote the requisite time to developing an awareness of who we really are.

Reflection

What heights am I capable of achieving?

_____

_____

_____

_____

What depths am I capable of descending to?

_____

_____

_____

_____

What do I notice when I stand outside myself and look within?

_____

_____

_____

_____

Which of the things I noticed do I identify with?

_____

_____

_____

_____

FUNCTION AND FORM

When speaking in terms of essence, it is easy to focus on the soul and forget that our body also plays an essential role. Each part has an integral function and needs to be employed properly. If we ignore either body or soul, we will be off track.

The Talmud expresses this message in the following anecdote:

> Antoninus said to Rebbi, "The body and soul can exempt themselves from any responsibility of wrongdoing. How so? The body can claim that it was the soul's fault – for from the day that the soul left me, I have been laying still like a stone in the grave. The soul can claim that it was the body's fault – for from the day that I left the body, I have been flying like a bird in the air."
>
> Rebbi replied: "Allow me to share with you a parable which will clarify the matter:
>
> "There was a king who had an orchard with beautiful fruit. He placed there two watchmen, one lame and one blind. The lame watchman said to the blind one, 'I see beautiful fruit in the orchard. Lift me on your shoulders so that we can gather and eat the fruit.' The blind watchman carried the lame one, and they ate the fruit.
>
> "After some time, the king returned to his orchard and asked, 'Where is my fruit?'
>
> "The lame watchman replied, 'Do I have legs to walk?'
>
> "The blind watchman answered, 'Do I have eyes to see?'
>
> "What did the king do? He placed the lame watchman on top of the blind one and judged them together. So too, G-d: He

brings the soul, throws it back into the body, and judges them together!"[1]

The faculties of the body and soul are watchmen of a beautiful orchard – man and his world. The difference between these watchmen is that the faculties of the body are blind, and those of the soul are sighted, but incapable of action without the body.

Our desire to remain alive pushes us to guard our health, and mobilizes every fiber in times of danger. Our desire for relationship moves us to set up homes and have children. Our desire to have the things others do pushes us to find a good livelihood. The love of our children pushes us to care for them and to raise them. All of these forces are amazing watchmen, which serve us and our world. To what end, though, is unknown. They are blind.

The sighted watchman is the soul. It can see a bigger picture and give our lives direction: To what aims should we aspire? Whom should we serve? What is worth acquiring?

The soul protects us from wasting our potential, and helps us to utilize our abilities for a purpose of value. The soul, however, is lame. It lacks the ability to carry out its will independently. For this, it needs the body.

Together, body and soul complete one another. The body provides function while the soul provides form. When they coexist in proper balance, both achieve their optimal state: The blind abilities of the body serve an elevated purpose, and the spiritual aspirations of the soul find expression in the world of action. But this is not always so simple.

We are designed to experience pleasure when we satiate an inner drive. From birth, we exist on a cycle: hunger, followed by appetite, followed by tasting food, followed by pleasure, followed by satiety, followed by the pleasure of being satisfied, and around again. This is true of other inner forces as well.

This pattern of hunger and satiety, need followed by pleasure, causes our imagination to be enjoyment-focused from its very inception. The appetite for food, which moves us to eat, was intended for the maintenance of our health. And at the same time, our imagination can get carried away. When this happens, pleasure instead of being a means, becomes an end in itself.

Pleasure as an end in itself invariably causes imbalance. The goal is

---

1. *Sanhedrin* 91a

not to uproot or negate our drives, but rather to watch over them, and maintain optimal balance. When we do this, our inner forces serve our well-being – protecting the garden of man, and keeping its fruit intact.

When we tend our garden with care, giving ample light and water as needed, and at the same time, keeping out the weeds, we will have a place of growth and beauty. Our trees will produce healthy and tasty fruit, which will benefit us and others. And they will continue to do so as long as we keep a watchful eye to make sure that proper equilibrium is maintained.

Reflection

What are some examples of how my soul fulfills its role?

_____

_____

_____

_____

What are some examples of how my body fulfills its role?

_____

_____

_____

_____

What are some things that would help my body and soul to be in better balance?

_____

_____

_____

_____

PERCEPTION AND PERSONALITY

It is tempting to think of our character traits as being similar to our other senses: seeing, hearing, feeling hungry, or being satiated. The appeal of this idea is that it absolves us of any responsibility to be different than we are. If we tend to be angry or impatient, well that is just how we are wired, and we are not to blame.

Maimonides, however, saw things differently. He referred to character traits as "deos"[1] – behavior patterns related to perception. This means that our character is affected by our viewpoint, and that by changing how we see things, we can likewise change our personality when in need of refinement.

The view of Maimonides, though, seems to be at odds with the Talmudic teaching that we are born with certain innate tendencies. For example, the Talmud states that a person born at a certain time of the year has a proclivity toward bloodshed, and recommends that people with this tendency channel their inclination in a positive way, such as by being a butcher or a mohel.[2, 3] Apparently, we are somewhat determined.

Similar to the question of, Are we a product of nature or nurture? both sides are true. Our personalities are both a product of innate forces as well as a function of our mind-set. Certain behavioral tendencies do exist, but how we channel them is up to us. And, to the degree that our conduct is dependent upon our outlook, we have the ability to change who we are.

1. Rambam, *Mishneh Torah*, Hilchos Deos
2. *Shabbos*, 156a
3. A mohel is one who performs circumcision.

The way to do this is by familiarizing ourselves with the lens through which we see the world. We do this by bringing our attention to our first-glance perceptions, noticing what our initial reactions are to different events. For example, the initial perspective of an angry person is that he should blow up at anyone who crosses or insults him. The initial perspective of an arrogant person is that others should praise and honor him. The initial perspective of a lazy person is that he should avoid any exertion in a positive direction.

In addition, each trait has a supporting cast of creative imagery, which precedes its associated behaviors. The angry person visualizes images of anger. The arrogant person visualizes receiving honor. The lazy person imagines all the impediments and dangers that positive action might entail.[4]

Generally, these imaginings have little basis in reality. If we would take the time to reflect on the contents of our minds, we might discover how mistaken some of our attitudes are. Halacha (knowledge of Jewish Law) and common sense together brighten our blind spots.[5] When we actively engage in them, their radiance allows us to see ourselves by the light of day.

When we see anger more clearly, it becomes apparent how off-target it is. Instead of gaining respect by pouring forth our wrath, we invite mockery and perhaps even hatred. Arrogance is likewise misguided – did we create our abilities? Laziness is a close intellectual cousin of these, with its imaginary fears, which would be laughable if not for the fact that we take them so seriously.

With practice and perseverance, it is possible to reshape the lens through which we see the world. We can choose in advance how we wish to be and respond to our life situations according to thought-out principles. The more we invest in ingraining within ourselves the changes we desire, the more successful our transformation will be.

One powerful method for promoting change is to use positive mental imagery. Instead of imagining pictures of anger, we can call to mind visions of kindness. Instead of imagining receiving honor, we can see ourselves treating others with the utmost respect. The more vividly we envision the scene, the deeper its impact will be.

Because we are able to refine our character, it is our responsibility to

---

4. *Mishlei*, 22:13
5. Chazon Ish, *Emunah Vebitachon*, chap. 3

do so. We are obligated to look at our lens on life and work to improve it. As the Vilna Gaon taught, "Man exists to refine his nature, and if not for this, why is he here?"[6]

Reflection

What are some attitudes which affect my behavior?

_____

_____

_____

_____

How do I feel that I should be treated by others and how does this impact my conduct?

_____

_____

_____

_____

How do I feel that I should treat others (perhaps those I perceive as being lower in status) and how does this influence my manners?

_____

_____

_____

_____

What are some things I can do to improve my lens on life?

_____

_____

_____

_____

6. *Peirush HaGra*, Mishlei, 4:13

THE BLESSING WITHIN

Human character runs very deep. Every trait is a hidden world containing great wisdom. To uncover this wisdom, we need to cultivate our wakefulness.

When we carefully observe our behavior for an extended period of time, it is possible to gain a picture of the majority of traits that affect us. With an attentive mind, we can take note of the traits which appear at the blink of an eye, and those which surface infrequently. Taking a personal inventory of which traits are active, and to what extent, can be very revealing.

The benefit of such knowledge is immense. Rabbi Yerucham Levovitz, in explaining the following verse, which discusses Jacob's blessing of his children at the end of his life, brings to light how essential such knowledge is:

"And these are the things which their father said unto them, and he blessed them, each person according to *his* blessing, did he bless them." Rashi[1] explains, "Each person according to their blessing" – the blessing that was to come upon each one in the future."[2]

Rabbi Levovitz comments:

> We need to understand the nature of the blessings that Jacob gave to his children. Each blessing was specific, according to the nature and character of each son. We learn about this quality of a blessing from the episode in which Jacob blessed the two sons of Joseph.
>
> Joseph wanted his father to give the blessing of the firstborn to his eldest son. His father responded, "I know, my son, I know . . .

---

1. An acronym for Rabbi Shlomo Yitzchaki
2. Parshas Vayechi, *Bereishis*, 49:28

nonetheless, his younger brother will become greater than him."

What was Jacob answering Joseph? Why could he not just give Joseph's oldest son the blessing he was asked to give?

The reason that Jacob was unable to change the order of the blessings was because each blessing is specific to the nature and ability of the person being blessed.

But, if this is so, what was the greatness of the different tribes and their progenitors? Their unique attributes were no more than the expression of an inborn nature. Joseph's ability to overcome great temptation and not be seduced by the wife of his master, and his brother Judah's ability to admit the truth publicly when he was in the wrong,[3] were no more than manifestations of innate character strengths.

Why does the Torah make such a big deal over their accomplishments? Why should Judah have merited becoming the progenitor of kingship for doing something which came to him naturally?

The Torah is revealing a vital insight about personal development: Only by protecting and developing our natural attributes can we realize our inborn greatness. Recognizing and actualizing our unique potential is no small matter. For this, a person rightfully deserves credit.[4]

There is a famous quote from Rebbe Zusha of Anipoli:

"When I get to the next world, I am not afraid of G-d asking me, 'Why were you not Abraham?' I am afraid of Him asking me, 'Why were you not Zusha?'

We each possess a unique attribute which is naturally on such a level of completion, that in relation to it, we cannot understand how others could stumble in that area. A person who is naturally very patient looks at someone who is always getting angry as if they are insane. At the same time, the angry person possesses a different strength, which, in relation to it, the patient person comes up short. Regarding such differences, a great Rosh Yeshiva[5] once expressed, "Do not hate your neighbor for having different faults than your own."

In creation there is always a balance. Just as each of us is blessed with a unique strength, so too, we are each challenged by a specific area of

---

3. Judah had sentenced his daughter-in-law to death for getting pregnant following the death of his son. Unbeknownst to Judah, she had disguised herself as a harlot and he, himself, had gotten her pregnant. Tamar communicated this to Judah discreetly so as not to embarrass him. He took full responsibility and publicly admitted that she had not done anything wrong, but rather he had, not seeing to her remarriage after his son had died, and that the child to be born was from him.

4. *Daas Chochma U'Mussar*, 1:103

5. Head of a Talmudic academy

weakness. Who we are was consciously engineered to fit our mission in life. This includes our strengths as well as our weaknesses. Through recognizing and exercising the power of our positive attributes, we can overcome the challenge of our negative ones and become our very best.

Someone who has come to recognize both their greatest strength and their greatest weakness has achieved something invaluable. They have identified the crux of their life's work. With a clear picture of who we are, which traits affect us, and to what degree, we have the comprehension necessary to pinpoint our potential and transform it into an actuality.

Reflection

In which areas do I experience the greatest strength?

_____

_____

_____

_____

In which areas do I experience the greatest challenge?

_____

_____

_____

_____

How can I use my strengths to deal with my challenges?

_____

_____

_____

_____

IMAGINATION

There were two brothers, Rebbe Elimelech and Rebbe Zusha, who became eminent spiritual leaders. In their youth they would wander from town to town like homeless beggars to develop the trait of humility. When they would come to the town of Ludmir, they would stay at the home of a poor Jew named Reb Aharon.

After they became famous, they visited Ludmir with a chariot drawn by horses and an entourage of Chassidim. When they got close to the town, a wealthy member of the community came out to greet them and invited them to stay in his home. The brothers answered that the man should go to the city ahead of them and they would come to the city on their own.

As was their custom, they went to the house of their poor friend, Reb Aharon. The wealthy man came to them with a complaint that he had invited them first. The brothers replied, "We are the same people we always were, and therefore should not change where we stay. The only thing which has changed is our horses and chariot, and because of them you invite us. Therefore, take the horses and chariot and host them."

Keeping sight of who we are even when circumstances change is a mark of greatness. Even when things stay the same, it is hard to see ourselves accurately. This difficulty is compounded by the efforts of our imagination.

If we think about it, we have a lot to gain by imagining ourselves to be other than who we really are. Any faults we may have can disappear in a cloud of smoke. And any attributes we desire can be instantly ours. If others do not yet appreciate how awesome we are, well, they are unfortunately lacking in perception. Imagination is the ultimate cure for any self esteem issues.

The only problem, or perhaps solution, is that somewhere, we know the difference. Our intellect wages war on our imagination and confronts us with reality. But not before large chunks of our lives have vanished into the thin air of fantasy.

If we are really unlucky, we can get stuck in an imaginary self. This occurs when a deep chasm exists between who we are and who we imagine ourselves to be. The divide is so great that we lose touch with who we ever were to begin with.

To avoid wasting our lives, it is imperative to try and see ourselves through the eyes of reality. Without this, it is easy to fall prey to living the life of someone we imagine, but who does not even exist. The self-aware person watches out for this shadow and strives to live life from an authentic place.

Reflection

What do I gain by imagining myself to be other than I am?

_____
_____
_____
_____

What do I lose?

_____
_____
_____
_____

What can I do to be more authentic?

_____
_____
_____
_____

SELF-DESTRUCTIVE BEHAVIOR

Aside from the detours that our imagination can take us on, there is another force, which can also get us off track. Sometimes we find ourselves engaging in negative behavior, and suddenly catch ourselves and wonder, How did I get myself into this? Whether it is speaking badly of others or getting angry, these are not things that our imagination draws us to. Nor are these things which are inherently pleasurable. If so, what is it that ensnares us? This force is known as the pull of the "Yetzer Hara."[1] It is like an inner riptide, which pulls us treacherously out to sea.

When a person engages in thoughtless negativity with no apparent gain, it is indicative of the hold this force has over them. As the Talmud teaches:

> Someone who tears their clothing, or breaks their vessels, or throws out money in anger, should be in your eyes as an idolater, for this is the tactic of the Yetzer Hara. Today it tells him to do one thing, and the next day it tells him to do something else. Until finally it tells him to serve idols, and he does that as well.[2]

This force of negativity is a category unto itself. The world was created with a balance between the forces of good and evil in order that man should have free will to choose between them. These forces exist in both the outer world and in our inner world. The tendency toward self-destructive behavior results from this negative force, which strives to bring us down by pushing us senselessly toward its dictates.

---

1. Literally translated as the "evil inclination," it is a self-destructive force, which tries to corrupt us from within.
2. *Shabbos*, 95b

Once we are aware of this force, we can invoke the powers of reason and good within ourselves to overcome it. Our Sages taught: "A person should continuously incite their Yetzer Tov[3] against their Yetzer Hara[4]" – Awaken our inner forces of goodness and conquer negativity, as Tanna D'Bei Yishmael taught: "If this disgusting force meets up with you, drag it to the house of study."[5] By physically moving ourselves closer to the wisdom of G-d, we gain the necessary strength to rise above the pull of negative impulses.

In a city near Peshischa, there was a man who went crazy. But his craziness was limited to one thing. He got it into his head that the General of the Army where he lived was Elijah the prophet, and the Governor was the Messiah. From day to day, this idea possessed him more and more. He would go around speaking about this from morning until night.

His family was naturally concerned, and decided to go with him to see the great Chassidic master, Rebbe Bunim of Peshischa. Perhaps this venerable Sage could help. When they came before the Rebbe, this man immediately told the Rebbe that in his city dwell both Elijah and the Messiah. The Rebbe asked the man, "Who are they?"

He answered, "They are the General of the Army and the Governor."

The Rebbe then asked, "And who am I?"

To which the man replied, "Your honor is the Rebbe."

"If so," questioned the Rebbe, "Is it possible that I, the Rebbe, do not know that in your city are to be found both Elijah the prophet and the Messiah?"

The man responded, "Your honor knows this as well. But you do not desire to reveal this matter to anyone."

"That being the case," answered the Rebbe, "You can also know this matter and still not reveal it to anyone, just like me. Therefore, I caution you from revealing this matter further."

The man stopped speaking about Elijah the prophet and the Messiah, and soon returned to his senses.

---

3. Literally the "good inclination," it is a healthy part of us, which pushes us toward vitality and well-being.
4. *Berachos*, 5a
5. *Kiddushin*, 30b

Reflection

What are some examples of how I get tangled up in negativity?

_____

_____

_____

_____

What is bringing me to this?

_____

_____

_____

_____

When I get caught up in negativity, what are some things that would help me to get to a better state?

_____

_____

_____

_____

THE WORLD OF I

To be authentically ourselves, we need to avoid the pitfalls of the imagination and the Yetzer Hara. And at the same time, this is insufficient. We also need to clarify what is the self that we are referring to when we say "I."

There are two fundamental forces that are included in the concept of "I": the first is known as the will. The second is our sensation of pleasure and pain.

The will is an incredibly powerful force rooted deep within our psyche. It precedes thought,[1] and moreover uses the vehicle of thought to express itself in the world. The will provides our lives with direction, guiding us through the decisions we make, and which in turn make us.[2]

The experience of pleasure and aversion to pain take the lion's share in the realm of human ambition. The giants of mussar[3] taught that a person's entire ambition from day one is to experience pleasure. Initially a person's enjoyment is purely physical. As one develops, so does their sense of pleasure. Recognition and praise from parents and peers, as well as material acquisition join the pleasure scope. If a person develops further, they rise above mundane pleasures and come to appreciate spirituality and ever deeper levels of spiritual pleasure.

We desire that which is sweet to us. The Hebrew word "arev," which means sweet, is also the root of the word for a mixture or combination. This connection hints at a fundamental truth: That which is sweet to us combines with who we are, being taken in and embraced. That which

---

1. *Leshem Shvo VeAchlama*, Hakdamos VeShearim, Shaar 4, chap. 3
2. *Sefer HaChinuch*, Mitzvah 99
3. Jewish ethicists

is not sweet to us, is pushed away with both hands. To an extent, we are what we enjoy. What happens when the force of will and the sense of pleasure and pain clash with one another?

There exists a higher faculty, completing our concept of "I" known as 'free choice.' This quality decides between these two forces. The will is essentially spiritual, whereas the sense of pleasure is naturally inclined toward physical enjoyment. Understandably, these forces tend to be at odds at times, which is where the "I" comes into the picture.[4]

These competing forces are inexorably intertwined, expressing the challenge of possessing a spiritual soul in a physical body. Free choice is the factor which determines which way the scales will tip; whether the power of will becomes a servant of one's physical wants, or whether the sense of pleasure becomes more refined, a vehicle of spirituality. The force we choose to identify ourselves with defines who we are.

There is a well-known story from the innovative Chassidic master, Rebbe Nachman of Breslov, about a turkey prince, which illustrates this point:

There was a king who had a son who believed he was a turkey. The prince would sit under the dining room table and peck at the food which fell from whomever was eating there. The king called many doctors and healers to try and help his son, but none were of any use. Finally, a wise man came and sat under the table with the prince.

He was also a turkey, he told the prince. The wise man showed the prince, little by little, that even though one is a turkey, one can still sit at a table, eat with silverware, get dressed up, and interact with people. Finally he rehabilitated the king's son.

This wise man understood a fundamental truth, which all the other experts had missed: We are limited in our actions and in our oppor-tunities to the extent that our identity is limited. If we believe that we are a turkey, we will be limited by what we think a turkey can do, until someone shows us how versatile a turkey can be.

4. *Alei Shur*, vol. 1, Shaar 3

Reflection

What are some examples of how my will expresses itself?

_____

_____

_____

_____

What are some things which are sweet to me?

_____

_____

_____

_____

How does my identity limit me?

_____

_____

_____

_____

How can I overcome this limitation?

_____

_____

_____

_____

TO CHOOSE OR NOT TO CHOOSE

Sensitivity to pain and pleasure, and a sense of will are both evident from a very young age. The faculty of choice, however, is distinct from these. It lies beyond the realm of instinct, and requires an intellectual sophistication, necessary in order to weigh and decide between different options. Without this maturity and mind development, choice does not begin.

If a child knows that they will be punished if they take some candy, yet they really want the candy, there will be a struggle between two inclinations: the desire for pleasure and the fear of punishment. Whichever one is stronger will win the struggle. The winning of one instinctive pull over another is not called choosing. Oftentimes, even those who possess greater maturity and intellectual sophistication act without the use of these faculties.

A thinking person needs to ask: How much do I actually use my free choice, and how often am I living in 'automatic pilot' mode, with various habits and inclinations leading my life?

It is theoretically possible to live an entire life without ever using the faculty of free choice. A person born with a mild temperament, and receiving a basic education on how to behave from their parents, who does not face any major life challenges, can go through life with a good name, without ever consciously choosing their path. While this is an extreme, when we look within, how often do we really exercise our capacity for free choice?

Really, it is no small matter to be a choosing being. When it comes to the realm of action, the faculty of choice has to compete with all the other forces at work within us: our upbringing, our natural inclinations, our habits, among many other factors which influence us. For this reason the Torah's commandment to "Choose life"[1] is no simple matter. It is because of this challenge that Rabbi Yona of Girondi[2] considers this attribute to be among the loftiest of spiritual levels.

Only through consistent effort can we really become choosing beings. Like other areas of spiritual growth, such as love or awe of the Creator, our growth in this area depends upon what we invest in it. It is worthwhile developing the ability to consciously choose, considering that the entire edifice of reward and punishment depends upon it.

Tremendous ramifications arise from such an understanding of free choice, in terms of how we relate to ourselves, and to others. Most people, in all fairness, should be perceived as if they are lacking free choice. Really, most of their actions are little more than a collage of nature, education, and habit, with a broad stroke of inclination thrown in for color.

Oftentimes we ask about another's behavior, "What were they thinking!?"

The correct answer, more often than not, is that they were not thinking. They were simply acting out an inner script, which was written long ago and likely by a mediocre author.

How often do we ask of ourselves, What was *I* thinking!?

Through learning to exercise the ability to choose, we can experience the qualitative difference between pleasures of the senses, and pleasures of the mind and soul. Consciously selecting the object of our delight elevates us. This mindfulness opens a gate inwards to a life of inner richness.

A story is told of the great Torah Sage Rabbi Akiva Eiger. A man in his town had left his wife and was refusing to give her a *get* [writ of divorce], which would free her from him. As the Rabbi of the town, Rabbi Eiger summoned the man before him to implore him to give his wife a get. The man was not budging. Rabbi Eiger quoted the Mishna in Kiddushin: "A woman is acquired [betrothed] in three ways: through money, contract, or relations. And she goes out [from being married] in two ways: Through being given a get, or through her husband dying." He told the man to take his choice. The man walked out on the Rabbi, and very shortly after, passed away.

Not all choices are so dramatic. But the choice between being a choosing being or not is no less significant. It is a choice between going through life awake or asleep, alive or dead.

1. *Devarim,* 30:19
2. *Shaarei Teshuva,* 3:17

Reflection

What are some examples of opportunities for free choice in my life?

_____

_____

_____

_____

What are some examples of pleasures of the senses I enjoy?

_____

_____

_____

_____

What are some examples of pleasures of the mind and soul which I enjoy?

_____

_____

_____

_____

What is the difference between these two types of pleasure?

_____

_____

_____

_____

DAAS

Becoming a choosing being is not something we arrive at instinctively. To achieve this attribute, we need to develop our daas. Daas is the wisdom of perception and integration. It allows us to discern between variables of greater and lesser quality and choose things of superior quality. This faculty lies at the core of having a healthy sense of self, possessing an "I" to be proud of.

When our "I" is an expression of daas, our will is exercised purposefully. Our selection of what is "sweet" is a conscious one, chosen with responsibility and intellectual maturity. The result is an ongoing transformation of potential into actuality.

Daas is the agency through which acquisition is affected. Without it, ownership is impossible, for if we do not possess ourselves, what meaning is there to anything else we may own? So, how do we acquire ourselves?

Through knowing who we are, and living according to that understanding. The Talmud in Nedarim expresses this point: "This [daas] is within – everything is within. This is not within – what is within?! This [daas] has been acquired – what is lacking? This has not been acquired – what has been acquired?!"[1]

Rabbeinu Tam elaborates further on the quality of daas:

> We see that our soul possesses a daas capable of learning everything in the world. It has another daas, higher than the first, through which it knows itself, and its knowledge of that knowing. This is

---

1. *Nedarim*, 41a

referred to as the daas of daas – in this daas we experience close-ness to G-d, blessed be He.[2]

Rabbeinu Tam is describing our ability to reach great levels of consciousness. When a person develops these abilities of knowing, knowing oneself, and being able to stand outside oneself and perceive one's very knowing, this touches a place very deep within the self. This place of depth is one's inner life source, which comes from G-d. To connect to this place is to connect to one's life source – G-d, blessed be He.

The first time the great Chassidic master, Rebbe Levi Yitzchok of Berditchev, went to visit the famed tzaddik, Rav Shmelke of Nikolsburg, and returned to his home, his father-in-law asked him, "What did you learn there?"

Rebbe Levi Yitchok replied, "I learned that there is a Creator of all existence."

His father-in-law called over the maidservant and asked her, "Do you know that there is a Creator of the world?"

She answered, "For sure."

Rebbe Levi Yitzchok responded, "She says. I know."

Reflection

What do I stand to gain by developing my daas?

_____

_____

_____

What are some things I can do to develop my daas?

_____

_____

_____

_____

What would help me to make better choices?

_____

_____

_____

2. *Sefer HaYashar*, end of the fifth gate

WEIGHTS AND MEASURES

Knowing ourselves is not a one-time experience. Being a person of daas requires us to return within, again and again, thinking and rethinking who we are. No other area is as susceptible to error. There are no precise measurements given by the Torah, spelling out for us exactly what to be. Rather, we must each weigh things, and decide upon which measures to take.

Maimonides sets forth as law the distancing from extremes. One who succeeds in walking the middle of the road is called a "Chachom," a person of integrated wisdom.[1] One who leans somewhat to one extreme, as a measure of caution from the opposite extreme is called a "Chossid" – a pious person.

How to measure exactly in between the extremes is no simple matter. This difficulty is compounded by a lack of clarity in discerning between positive and negative traits as well. Many actions can be viewed in a number of ways. An enthusiastic greeting could be an expression of kindness or empty flattery; of good-heartedness or deceit.

Furthermore, we naturally judge ourselves favorably, narrowing our vision to block out any negative traits. At the same time, we may suffer from complete blindness when it comes to seeing our positive traits. Being intelligent people, we may realize that we are not angels, and succeed in recognizing our faults. Yet, when we fail to acknowledge our natural strengths, the self-picture we carry will be tragically inaccurate.

Really, our faults are easier to spot. They rear their heads often, attempting to express themselves in myriad ways. Our strengths are often-

1. *Mishneh Torah*, Hilchos Deos, 1:4

times more subtle and refined, requiring greater sensitivity and aware-ness to perceive.

In addition, the tendency to find fault in others acts as a double-edged sword. When we are quick to see others with a negative eye, we establish a pattern of looking for lacking. As a result, when it comes to ourselves, our powers of judgment have been corrupted and we are unable to see our own good points.

The saintly Chafetz Chaim used to make a daily spiritual account-ing. He would seclude himself in his attic and sometimes spend several hours there. Earlier in his life he had been a storekeeper and had been in charge of keeping the books, making sure that all the accounts were in order. He reasoned that if in mundane matters one has to be so care-ful, making a regular accounting, all the more so in matters of the soul.

Making time for a spiritual accounting is necessary if we care about the contents of our personal inventories. Being aware of what is there and what is missing allows us to stay on top of our personal business. And like in business, accurate bookkeeping can make all the difference between success and failure.

Reflection

What are some examples of where I tend to extremes?

_____

_____

What are some areas where I am more balanced?

_____

_____

If I would make a spiritual accounting what would my credits be?

_____

_____

_____

What would my debits be?

_____

_____

BEWARE OF LABELS

As we get more in touch with our inner inventories, we need to be careful about labeling our middos. Different terms that we have heard of, or come across in our readings, pop into mind. It can be very tempting to assign labels to our various parts and file them away for safekeeping.

Why do we do this?

Part of the reason is that uncertainty is uncomfortable. It is easier to label and file our personalities, rather than deal with uncertainty, especially about ourselves.

The value of labeling, however, can be overestimated. One can know themselves deeply and accurately even if they lack the appropriate vocabulary to describe all their different traits. This does not mean that having a rich vocabulary to describe inner processes is a problem. On the contrary, it can help us get a better handle on our inner world. But, the inner knowledge is the goal – not the assignment of labels.

Daniel was repeatedly referred to by his teacher in elementary school as "lazybones." In his early thirties, despite being quite intelligent and charming, he had trouble following through on any project he became involved with. He explained, "Well, I guess I am just lazy. Even my teacher in elementary school said so and nicknamed me lazybones." Daniel had so identified with this label that he had difficulty seeing himself in any way that was inconsistent with it.

Once a label is used, it can take on a life of its own. This life can be sadly limited. As a result, we need to exercise the greatest caution when using labels.

Reflection

What labels have been used to describe me?

_____

_____

_____

_____

How accurate have these labels been?

_____

_____

_____

_____

How have these labels impacted me?

_____

_____

_____

_____

What labels do I use when referring to myself?

_____

_____

_____

_____

CHILDHOOD MEMORIES

When exploring our inner world, we would be remiss if we did not consider how it has been shaped by our childhood. It is during these formative years that our personality traits are largely formed. Therefore, if we aspire to arrive at a deep knowledge of ourselves, we need to consider what our experience of those years was like.

The patterns of how we relate to ourselves and others, more often than not, owe their origin to childhood experiences. When we recall the games we played, and our imaginings; our beginnings in thought and in having a place in the world; our fears and our loves – we acquire a vital key toward understanding the person we are today.

The Talmud expresses the centrality of childhood in the fabric of life:

"There are those who say: 'Fortunate is our childhood that it did not embarrass our maturity' – these are the pious ones and those great in acts. And there are those who say: 'Fortunate is our maturity, which has atoned for our childhood' – these are the baalei teshuva.[1]"[2]

The Talmud is discussing the great joy experienced by the Jewish people during the Simchas Beis HaShoeva (special water libation ceremony during the Sukkot Holiday). This was the highest point of joy in the Jewish year, the time when there was a 'drawing forth' of the Divine Spirit. What was the focal point of this joy? How their lives had fared vis-à-vis their childhood.

Two great Chassidic masters made a match between their children. One of the Rebbes (Chassidic leaders) got up by the engagement ceremony and, as was his custom at such an occasion, went through the

---

1. People who have turned their lives around, to come close to G-d
2. *Sukkah,* 53a

history of his family and their ancestry. His list included some of the greatest Chassidic personalities of past generations.

When he was done, he invited his future in-law to recount his ancestry as well. The other Rebbe got up and said, "When I was ten years old, I lost both my parents, and do not remember them well enough to tell their praise. But this I know, that they were whole and straight in their hearts.

"When I became an orphan, a relative apprenticed me to a tailor to learn his trade. I spent five years with him and was a faithful worker. Even though I was young, I learned to always be careful in two things: Not to ruin the new, and to fix the old."

The other Rebbe understood the message, and was moved by the depth evident in the words of his future in-law. Illustrious lineage only has value to the extent that it informs our present lives. This orphan, who later became a Rebbe, had learned a life lesson of priceless value from his own "lineage": Not to ruin the new, and to fix the old. The match was sealed in joy.

Reflection

What are some examples of childhood experiences which shaped me?

_____

_____

_____

_____

What are some parallels between who I was as a child and who I am today?

_____

_____

_____

_____

What are some life lessons that my childhood taught me?

_____

_____

_____

_____

JOURNALING

Rabbi Kalonymus Kalman Shapira poignantly expresses the sentiment of a person who has worked his entire life to get to a higher place, only to realize that once there, life is soon over. He offers a piece of constructive advice, considering these circumstances:

Wouldn't it be great if we could live another seventy years after our time here is up. We spend an entire lifetime working on ourselves, trying to refine and elevate who we are. If we had another lifetime, then we could live a higher type of existence, even in this world. But, after a life filled with difficult challenges, all of a sudden we are gone. G-d has taken us.

This being the case, it would be good to give written form to our thoughts. Not for the sake of writing a book, but rather to imprint oneself upon paper, to concretize all that we go through, our ups and our downs. In doing so, our essence, our form, and our development throughout life will remain alive. Those who learn and internalize our life lessons give continuity to our time here, even after we are gone, carrying our legacy forth into eternity.[1]

Aside from the motive of leaving a legacy, journaling is a powerful tool for self-awareness and development. As we give our thoughts written form, we gain greater clarity into our own life experiences. As time passes and we keep on writing, a sharper picture of who we are, and who we are becoming, emerges. If such clarity is important to us, we need to take the time to journal.

---

1. *Tzav Veziruz*, Rav Kalonymus Kalman Shapira

Reflection

What life lessons would I want to be part of my legacy?

_____

_____

_____

_____

What challenges would I want my readers to know about and learn from?

_____

_____

_____

_____

What benefits would I have from making journalling a part of my life?

_____

_____

_____

_____

DISSECTING AN ACTION

The days of our lives are defined by our actions. To understand the quality of our deeds, we need to better appreciate the varied faculties which join together to bring an action into actuality. The basic outline is that first, a stimulus occurs, which awakens different traits. Subsequently, a chain of inner movement is set into motion. And finally, this process culminates in action. To better understand ourselves and the things we do, we need to take apart this progression, from beginning to end.

The Torah, in several instances, teaches us how to dissect an action.

When the Jews were in the desert, Moses' cousin, Korach, staged a rebellion. He was upset at being passed over for the appointment of leader of his clan and expressed his chagrin by questioning Moses' leadership, and the appointment of Moses' brother, Aaron, as the high priest. He posed to Moses, together with a large following, several seemingly intellectual challenges, with the goal of undermining Moses' authority.

If we look closely at Korach's opposition to Moses, we find a number of variables:

1. Korach's claim: "The entire assembly is holy, and within them is G-d, and why are you raising yourself above the community of G-d?"

The Midrash Tanchuma gives a fuller accounting of the questions which Korach asked Moses:

"A Tallis [fringed garment] which is completely techeiles [blue] colored, does it need a string of techeiles to exempt it from the obligation of tzitzis?! A house full of sefarim [books of Torah study], does it need a mezuzah?![1] And a congregation which is all holy, do they need a leader?!"

---

1. Handwritten scroll of "Hear O Israel," placed on the doorposts of entrances in Jewish homes.

Korach was advocating an entire philosophy on the nature of the commandments, and the function of a leader. He was challenging the entire basis of Moses's leadership as being from G-d, in addition to there being any hierarchy whatsoever within the Jewish people. His claim was that we are all holy, we all experienced revelation. And if you, Moses, are lifting up some people above others, you made that up yourself.

2. Our Sages asked: "Korach was extremely intelligent; what did he see to get involved in this stupidity? [There was very clear evidence of Moses' authority and the concept of a hierarchy within the Jewish people.] They answer: His eye caused him to err. He saw with divine spirit that a chain of greatness was destined to come forth from him, referring to the prophet Samuel, who was considered equal in a certain respect to Moses and Aaron. He said to himself, "Because of him I will get away." His faulty thinking grabbed on to a point of holiness – the future greatness that would descend from him, which he saw with divine spirit, and which led him to believe that he would be successful in his campaign.

3. "What brought Korach to oppose Moses? He was jealous of the appointment of Elitzafan the son of Uziel, whom Moses had appointed as leader over the Kehatites, according to G-d's instruction."[2] The spark which ignited the fire was the appointment of Korach's cousin to leadership and not him.

4. "He was jealous."[3] This was the basis of the entire episode. This was the trait which was awakened by the appointment of Korach's cousin as tribal leader.

The Torah here outlines the layers of process beneath our behavior. A trait is first awakened, in this case, the jealousy of Korach. It then takes hold of a point of holiness – the vision of greatness which would descend from him. Finally, a "philosophy" is formed, justifying, and even obligating the acts of Korach.[4]

Another example of this pattern is found in the episode of the Meraglim (the spies who went to scout out the land in preparation for the Jews entering into the land of Israel following the receiving of the Torah, and who reported against it). The spies claimed, "We cannot go up to the nation, for it is mightier than us." They grabbed on to the actuality: "It is a land which consumes its inhabitants. Every place we walked, the inhabitants were burying the dead."

2. Rashi, Parshas Korach, 16:1
3. Ibid.
4. *Alei Shur*, vol. 1, pp. 160–161

The Sages reveal to us the spies' primary motivation in speaking against the land of Israel: they were about to come into the land of Israel, and there was a possibility that leadership would change (and they would lose their positions of greatness). The traits awakened within them were the desire for power, and jealousy of those who might rise to leadership in place of them. After these traits were awakened, destructive words soon followed.

A third example is found in the episode of Shechem (in which Simeon and Levi, the sons of Jacob, killed an entire city following the abduction and abuse of their sister Dina by the prince of the city). The actuality: Dina was defiled. The philosophy: Responsibility to avenge their sister's honor, stemming from brotherhood. The underlying trait, however, is revealed by their father Jacob: Anger! " . . . in your anger you killed."[5]

The above examples demonstrate that action is a product of middos (character traits). The philosophy or rationalization upon which acts are predicated is an effect of the middah (trait), created to justify or even obligate its acts. Pure philosophy does not exist. It always draws upon the wellspring of middos.

Once we realize how deeply our middos affect our judgment, we need to carefully examine the reasons we give to validate our actions. When middos are involved, and they are always involved, we need to be aware of the prejudices they create, which often result in falsehood. If we are aware of this, we stand a greater chance of retaining some objectivity and making fewer mistakes.

G-d had performed a kindness for the Meraglim. He made the inhabitants of the land busy, burying their dead, so that they would not notice the spies. If the Meraglim had perceived things correctly, they would have recognized G-d's kindness. Instead, their own issues got involved and they read the situation completely backwards, bringing sorrow upon the entire nation.

We are endowed with an intellect which allows us to rationalize just about anything. As a result, it is necessary to check what lies behind our reasoning aside from pure logic. By looking at the situation we find ourselves in, and taking stock of the character traits which may have been aroused, we have a much better chance of judging things accurately.

---

5. Parshas Vayechi

Reflection

What are some of my life philosophies?

_____

_____

_____

_____

What are some examples of how these philosophies are expressed in action?

_____

_____

_____

_____

How have these philosophies been influenced by my life events and subsequent character traits?

_____

_____

_____

_____

What helpful adjustments can I make to my philosophies?

_____

_____

_____

_____

REFRAME

It is amazing that despite our proximity to ourselves, it can be so hard to see ourselves clearly. Part of the reason is that we do not want to. We are afraid to see some lacking we do not like, which would make it difficult for us to feel good about ourselves. Instead, we find it is easier to relate to ourselves as strangers, ignorant of who we really are.

Paradoxically, it is our willingness to examine the areas in which we are lacking which can lift us up. The fact that we can recognize and are bothered by a weakness in some area means that we are sensitive to the positive attribute or value which is missing. If we had no connection to the value or attribute, its absence would not bother us. We probably would not even notice it.

The experience of feeling a lacking in an attribute testifies to the connection we have to that strength. If we value wisdom, we will feel that the wisdom we have acquired is insufficient and incomplete. If we value kindness, we will feel that we could be kinder. It is our appreciation of the positive which engenders the sensitivity we have toward an absence of it.

Live skin feels the cut of a knife. Dead skin does not. If we are alive to wisdom, or any other positive quality, we will feel when it is missing. If, on the other hand, we feel that in some area we have already filled our cups and are complete, as far as that area is concerned, we are dead.[1]

Instead of getting discouraged when we notice a lack of completeness in some attribute, we can feel encouraged. Our ability to feel bothered by something missing testifies to our being alive and connected to that attribute. When we appreciate this, seeing our lacking becomes much

1. Maharal, *Be'er HaGolah*, Hakdamas HaMechaber

less frightening, and we are able to feel encouraged instead of discouraged by perceiving the areas in which we have room to grow.

Reflection

Which areas of lacking bother me?

_____

_____

_____

_____

What does this say about me?

_____

_____

_____

_____

What are some things I can do to grow in the attribute(s) which I value?

_____

_____

_____

_____

CIRCUMSTANCE

Environment profoundly impacts what our values are. Each set of circumstances influences our middos differently, including the ideas which stem from those middos. When putting ourselves in a situation, we need to be conscious of which middos are likely to be awakened[1] so that we can perceive the thoughts which cross our minds with the necessary objectivity.

King Solomon, the wisest of all men, taught in Proverbs, "And you shall eat and be satiated and deny, saying, 'Who is G-d?'" King Solomon is warning: Beware of the state of satisfaction.[2] It can lead to rebelling against G-d.

When we are less satisfied, we are more inclined to turn toward G-d. Feeling more humble, we look to Him to fill our lacking. Once we are satisfied, however, we are in danger of stumbling if we do not guard ourselves from smugness.

The Jewish people sinned with the golden calf. Moses argued in their defense that the abundance of gold and silver that G-d had given them had led them to stray. The yeshiva of Rabbi Yanai figuratively expressed: A lion does not roar from a box of hay, but rather from a box of meat.

Rabbi Yochanan gave the following parable to clarify Moses' defense of the Jewish people:

A man had a son. He bathed him and anointed him, fed him and gave him to drink, hung a purse of money from his neck, and placed him in front of a house of ill repute – What can the son do except sin!?[3] It was

1. *Daas Torah*
2. Rashi, *Devarim*, Parshas Eikev, 11:16
3. *Berachos*, 32a

the circumstance of the Jews' being given incredible wealth upon leaving Egypt that caused their downfall!

Maimonides wrote that it is the nature of man to be drawn after the people around him in attitude and in action. He must, therefore, choose his environment with the utmost care.[4] Whether we like it or not, we are affected by the circumstances we find ourselves in.

The great Chassidic master, the Chidushei HaRim, taught this lesson on the day that he first entered the new house of study in Gur:

He quoted the following piece of Talmud: On the day that Rabban Gamliel had been removed from his position as leader of the Jewish people, the guard at the entrance of the house of study was removed, and permission was given to all the students to enter.[5] Previous to that day, Rabban Gamliel had decreed that any student whose insides did not match their outside appearance (of being a Torah scholar) may not enter the house of study. Following the removal of Rabban Gamliel from his post, a number of benches were added to the house of study to accommodate all the new students. Rabban Gamliel felt remorse over the policy he had established. Rashi explains that he was worried about deserving punishment for having prevented all these students from coming to the house of study in his days.

The Chiddushei HaRim asked: What did Rabban Gamliel understand now that he had not understood before, that caused him to worry and retract from his original position of not allowing students to enter whose insides did not match their outsides?

He answered that when these students whose insides did not match their outsides came to the house of study, the influence of the house of study was so powerful that it immediately transformed them into students whose insides did match their outsides. Rabban Gamliel sensed this and felt sorry at having prevented these students from coming in the past. He understood that had he let them in, it would have positively influenced them.

4. *Mishneh Torah*, Hilchos Deos, 6:1
5. *Berachos*, 28a

Reflection

What are a few examples of how different situations have brought out different things in me?

_____

_____

_____

_____

How do my present circumstances impact me?

_____

_____

_____

_____

What are some ways that I can use the power of environment to my benefit?

_____

_____

_____

_____

PROJECTION

We often see others, and the world around us, not as they are, but as we are. Our inner worlds include an entire realm of thought and emotion, and the dividing line between what lies within and what lies without is not always so clear. At times this inner world breaks forth into our consciousness, bringing feelings of fear and anger, sadness or apathy, and even joy or euphoria. And frequently we do not even know why.

How can we better understand what lies inside so that we can discern what is from within, and what is from without?

The Torah provides several suggestions for broadening our lens of self awareness:

In the area of Torah study, the Talmud Yerushalmi taught, "For there is nothing empty, and should you find emptiness, it is from you."[1]

We sometimes reach an "empty" point in Torah. No content or necessity is clearly visible in the matter at hand. This perception is a red flag, waving at a specific facet of inner emptiness. Something in our spirituality is missing, and that lacking is being projected onto the Torah.

For example, a scholar of ability plumbs the depths of Talmudic debates, yet when he comes upon areas of Torah requiring emotional sensitivity (such as Aggadata – deep allegorical teachings), he skips over them, seeing nothing noteworthy. Something is missing. If this scholar could open his eyes and read the lack of writing on the walls, he might be open to doing some inner work. If he would do so, he would become a much greater Torah scholar and human being (the two are inseparable).

The Torah also addresses the tendency to project one's inner content,

---

1. *Talmud Yerushalmi*, Peah 1:1

or lack thereof, elsewhere in the case of the Meraglim. Following their evil report of the land, the Jewish people said, "Because of G-d's hatred for us, He took us out of Egypt, to place us into the hands of the Emorites, to destroy us."[2] Rashi comments on the words, "Because of G-d's hatred for us" – "And G-d loved them – but you hated Him."[3] As the adage says: That which is in your heart, you say about the other; that which is in his heart, he says about you.

Within the heart of the Jews who lived in the desert there lay a subtle point of hatred toward G-d (relative to their great spiritual level). They would never admit this, even to themselves, being largely unaware of this hidden sentiment. Nonetheless, their emotional reality was revealed through the projection of their feelings onto G-d.

The mistaken thinking of these Jews caused them great suffering. In their minds' eye, they saw themselves as lovers of G-d, following Him with all their hearts. At the same time, they perceived themselves as having lost favor with G-d, and having been cast out for destruction.

These thoughts began and ended with themselves and had no basis in reality. All their pain and sorrow was the product of their own minds. The only truth which was revealed, and with precision, was the content of their own hearts. "That which is in your own heart, you say about the other . . . !"[4]

Another powerful example of this phenomenon is found in Jewish Law. Maimonides wrote in his code of law: " . . . whoever finds fault in others, constantly denigrating families or individuals because of their lineage, calling them 'mamzerim' (born from a forbidden relationship) – we suspect him of being a 'mamzer.' And if he calls them slaves – we suspect him of being a slave.[5] For whosoever renders others deficient does so with their own deficiency."[6]

It must be that the person casting aspersions is unaware of their own blemish. If they were aware, they would be more careful, so as not to reveal their own shame. Whether they never really knew, or simply forgot, within the heart nothing is forgotten. Eventually, the tendency to project outwards reveals to all what lies within.

Being aware of this, we should be wary of making critical statements about others. Quite possibly, our negativity says much more about us

2. *Devarim*, 1:27
3. Rashi, ibid.
4. Rashi, ibid.
5. *Mishneh Torah*, Hilchos Issurei Biah, 19:17
6. *Kiddushin*, 70a

than it does about anyone else. At the same time, this tendency to criticize others with our own faults has great value in terms of self-discovery. When we feel a desire to level some criticism at someone, we can examine our critique and pinpoint where we, ourselves could use some work. Instead of using fault-finding as a weapon with which to harm others, we can use it as a tool with which to recognize and repair ourselves.

There was a young man from the city of Apta, who was a G-d-fearing Torah scholar. Unfortunately, he was ordered to enlist in the Russian army. This was a disaster on many levels. In the Russian army, living in accordance with the Torah was prohibitively difficult, aside from all the hardships a young Jewish man would endure there for many years. The father of this young man was a simple Jew who worked hard to eke out a living and he lacked the necessary means to pay off the authorities.

At the time, the Rabbi of the city was the famous Chassidic Rebbe, the Ohev Yisrael. One Friday, when the Rabbi was in the bath house, he went out to the outer change room to rest. Some leading members of the community were there and the Rebbe began to speak to them, arousing their hearts to help this young man and redeem him from having to go to the army. The men were moved by the Rebbe's words and were willing to help redeem the young man from being conscripted into the army. But then, one of them said, "I don't know why the Rebbe is going to such lengths to redeem this young man, the son of so-and-so. Who will miss him if he is not here? Will our city no longer be a city?"

Once the words had left this man's lips, the other men lost interest in helping the young Torah scholar. The Rebbe's face reddened and he got up and left them, returning to the bath house. The man who had spoken put on his clothes and left the bath house. On his way home, an ox gored him and he was brought home in his death throes.

When it became known to this man's household that he had offended the Rebbe, they went to appease him. They met him as he was leaving the bath house. The Rebbe said to them, "G-d forbid, I did not punish him, nor did I pray that he should be punished, especially not in the bath house, where it is forbidden to pray. But truthfully, I have to tell you that at the moment he said his words, 'And if so-and-so is missing from the city, will our city no longer be a city?' I had the following thought: If this man is missing from the city will our city no longer be a city? And with all my strength, I tried to drive this thought from my mind, but was unable to. What can I do if the matter was decreed from above?"

Reflection

What are some critical statements that I have made about others?

_____

_____

_____

_____

What do my comments say about me?

_____

_____

_____

_____

PRAISE

"... And a person according to their praise."[1]

When we want to know the quality of silver and gold; how good it is, what is true weight, and what is dross; the metal is smelted and the impurities are burnt out until it is pure. Likewise, our own quality can be discerned according to our praise. The way that we are praised by others reveals who we are.[2]

The Chafetz Chaim was involved in a court case. In his defense, someone told the judge a tale about this great man. The story portrayed the great saintliness of the Chafetz Chaim. Upon hearing the story, the judge said to the lawyer, "I do not know if the story is true, but they do not tell such stories about you and I."

How we are praised is very revealing. Yet, when it comes to using this as a tool to learn about ourselves, it is a bit inaccessible. Generally, there is a discrepancy between what is said in front of us and what is said in our absence.

There is another explanation of the verse, "and a person according to their praise," which is much more useful as a tool for self-knowledge. Rabbi Yona of Girondi explains: A person who praises good acts, and the wise and the righteous ... we know that he is a good person. Whereas, one who praises lowly behavior or evildoers proclaims what type of a person he is.[3]

Listening to what comes out of our mouths and hearing the subject of our praise tells us a lot about who we really are. If our values are repre-

1. *Mishlei,* 27:21
2. Metzudas Dovid, *Mishlei,* 27:21
3. *Shaarei Teshuva,* Shaar 3, p. 148

sented in our praise, we know where we stand. But if there is a disparity between what we claim to value and what we hear ourselves praising, we need to reexamine what it is we really value.

Reflection

What do I hear my lips praising?

_____

_____

_____

_____

What does this say about me?

_____

_____

_____

_____

What would I like to adjust?

_____

_____

_____

_____

SIGHT

The Talmud entertains the possibility that just by looking at an owner-less object we can acquire it.[1] How does this make any sense? How can simply looking at something bring it into our domain?

When we consider how sight works, we can appreciate where the Talmud is coming from. Sight depends upon the existence of a light source. Light emits rays, which bounce off objects and then reach our eye. Once these light particles pass through the surface of the eye, they travel through several layers, setting off nerve pulses, which are sent to the optic nerve, which sends these pulses to our brain, where an image is formed.

On a physical level, we are coming into contact with the object of our focus. With our sight, we are touching it and bringing it into our personal domain. Once we understand this, it is not such a jump to consider the possibility that ownership could be accomplished by look-ing at an object.

Whatever exists on a physical plane exists on a spiritual plane as well. Looking at something or someone forges a spiritual connection in ad-dition to the physical one. This explains the injunction of our Sages not to look into the face of a morally corrupt person.[2] Looking at such a person attaches us to their negativity. By the same token, gazing at the countenance of a spiritually elevated person lifts us up.[3]

The Vilna Gaon, one of the greatest Torah scholars of the past several hundred years, was once accused of a crime against the government.

---

1. *Bava Metziah*, 118a
2. *Megillah*, 28a
3. *Shem MiShmuel*, Vayishlach, 5681

He was put into jail, where he awaited his court case. The lawyer who was given the task of defending him came into his cell and the Vilna Gaon averted his gaze from the man. The lawyer, taking offense, said to the Vilna Gaon, "Don't you know that it is up to me to defend you!?" The Vilna Gaon calmly replied, "It makes no difference. Our Sages have ruled that it is prohibited to gaze upon the face of a corrupt person."

At the court case, the Judge, after reading the charges, asked the lawyer to respond. The lawyer replied, "Your honor, it is impossible that this man committed the crime he is accused of. Even though he knows that it is my job to defend him, he refuses to even look at me because of my own moral standing. Such a person could not have performed such a crime." The Judge was impressed and dismissed the charges.

Standing in a room full of people, we may notice how differently we feel as we glance at each face. Every face is a window into a world of distinctive quality. Therefore, the experience of connecting to each world differs.

Being aware of how sight affects us allows us to use it to greater advantage. By focusing on material of higher substance, and limiting the amount of garbage we allow in, we can improve the content of our inner world. How much or how little, is up to us.

Rabbi Elimelech Menachem Mendel of Strikov once asked his followers, while he was teaching Torah during the festive meal of Sabbath night, to pray from a Siddur (prayer book). He explained: When we go out into the world to earn our livelihoods, we see all sorts of things which affect us negatively, and are not even aware of the impact these things have on us. But, when we pray from the Siddur, seeing the holy letters invests our sight with their holiness. This, in turn, awakens our hearts not to look at things which are detrimental to us.

Reflection

What are some examples of things that impact me when I see them?

_____

_____

_____

_____

How do these things impact me?

_____

_____

_____

_____

What are some things that it would be healthy to see less of?

_____

_____

_____

_____

What are some things it would be healthy to see more of?

_____

_____

_____

_____

FINGERS AND EARS

The Talmud[1] asks a seemingly strange question: Why are fingers angled like pegs?

The Talmud answers: So that if a person hears something which is improper, he can place his fingers in his ears.

This give and take sounds a bit odd. What wisdom are the Sages of the Talmud coming to impart with this question and answer?

The ear is physically open to hearing anything within earshot. Whatever goes in has the ability to shape and influence the person that is listening to its message. A person who is open to everything and anything is lacking a defined inner form.

The dexterity our fingers possess, in addition to their shape, allows us to create magnificent works of intricate detail. Man was endowed with the faculty of free choice in order to create a masterpiece – himself – which would possess an incredible quality of positive detail. He was entrusted with no less a task than being a partner in his own creation.[2]

Our Sages are revealing a deep connection between the concepts of our fingers and our ears. They are teaching that a person of form takes action to ensure that the material he uses to mold himself with should be of the highest quality, filtering out that which is unworthy. When we exercise discernment, the product that we shape is quite different from the product of those who let everything into their world.

A Chassid once came to his Rebbe complaining bitterly about the impure thoughts which plagued his mind. He asked the Rebbe what he could do to free himself of these thoughts. The Rebbe told the Chassid,

1. *Kesubos*, 5a
2. *Vayikra Rabbah*, 35:7

"In the middle of the forest, next to our town, there is a little house. Go there and knock on the door. Perhaps the person who lives there can help you."

The Chassid walked through the forest until he finally found the house. He came to the door and knocked, but no one answered. He continued knocking, first a little louder, and then with all his might, but no one came to the door. Finally, dejected, he left and came back to the Rebbe to tell him what had happened. Upon hearing the Chassid's report, the Rebbe replied, "You see, just because someone knocks on your door does not mean that you have to open it . . ."

Reflection

What are some examples of things I hear which impact me?

_____

_____

_____

_____

How do these things impact me?

_____

_____

_____

_____

What are some things it would be beneficial to hear less of?

_____

_____

_____

_____

What are some things it would be helpful to hear more of?

_____

_____

_____

_____

TASTE

We are all connoisseurs of our own life experiences. We possess an innate sense of what tastes good to us and what does not. We are able to detect fine nuances of flavor in the varied happenings of our day, some more palatable, and some less.

When describing behavior, we may refer to something as having been in "poor taste." A joke may be "tasteless." An event which really hits the mark may be spoken of as having been in good, or even excellent, taste.

Why do we describe behavior or experiences in terms of palate?

We live a multi-layered existence. That which exists in the highest spiritual worlds also exists in a lower form in our world. Because of this interconnection, we can understand higher concepts through comparison to lower concepts. For example, the concept of an eye, below, which is the organ of sight, corresponds to the concept of Divine providence above. G-d is watching us, as it were, through "His eyes."[1]

In this world, as well, we use similar language to describe different levels. A person who has lifted themselves spiritually may be referred to as an elevated person. So too, one who has climbed to the top of a hill is also elevated. Despite the fact that we are talking about two very different things, there is a conceptual commonality between them, which brings us to talk about them in the same terms.

We use the word "taste" when talking about food and similar items. We also use the term "taste" when speaking of how sensible something is. In Biblical Hebrew the word for "reason" and the word for "taste" is one and the same – "taam." In the Talmud, one of the most frequently asked questions is, "What is the taam [What is the reason for . . .]?"

---

1. Ramchal, *Daas Tevunos*, Siman 80

Superficially, taste and reason are two completely different things. But, when we take a deeper look, we see that they are really the same thing. Through a thing's taste, we come into closer contact with it and can discern its quality.[2] So too, on an intellectual level, when we delve into the reasoning behind something, looking at it from all angles, wrapping our head around it, we come into intimate contact with it and experience a felt sense of its quality.[3] We can taste it.

When something makes sense to us, we want to absorb it. It has taste. When something is unreasonable, we reject it. It lacks taste, or has a bad taste.

As we go through life, we may sometimes experience things which taste "off." Instead of just going on, we need to stop and ask ourselves, what is the reason that this experience is unpalatable? What is not making sense here?

Conversely, when something does taste good, it would be worth our while to ask ourselves, What about this is making sense? By doing so, we know what to look for and can experience this flavor more often, increasing the quality of our lives.

Rebbe Yehuda served Antoninus (the Roman Emperor) a meal on the Sabbath. Antoninus enjoyed it very much. During the week, Antoninus made a similar meal and found it to be lacking. He commented on this to Rebbe Yehuda. Rebbe Yehuda answered, "Your food preparers are missing one spice." Antoninus questioned, "Is the king's kitchen lacking for anything?!" Rebbe Yehuda responded, "They are missing the Sabbath. Does your kitchen have that?"[4]

Reflection

What are some things which I find to be in poor taste?

_____

_____

_____

_____

2. *Yoreh Deah*, Siman 98, *Taz, Beis, Mishbetzos Zahav*
3. *Shiurei Daas*, vol. 1, p. 38
4. *Bereishis Rabbah*, 11:4

What are some examples of things which have been in excellent taste?

_____

_____

_____

_____

What are some tastes I would like to experience more often in my life?

_____

_____

_____

_____

What are some things I can do to make this happen?

_____

_____

_____

_____

WORDS

The Torah is very economical in its use of words. Many laws are derived from a single letter or a seemingly slight nuance in language. At the same time, when describing an impure animal, the Torah adds eight letters[1] to avoid saying "impure."[2] Instead, it refers to a certain type of animal as, "the animal which is *not pure*" (in Biblical Hebrew the difference is eight letters).

What would we have lost had the Torah simply referred to the animal as "impure"? Rabbi Yehoshua ben Levi explains that the Torah is imparting a lesson in the use of speech: A person should protect his lips from allowing a lowly utterance to pass through them. If the Torah spent eight extra letters to avoid using a negative term, we should likewise go the extra mile in avoiding negativity in our speech.

A teacher and his students were traveling together and came across the carcass of an animal. The students commented on how bad the animal smelled. Their teacher countered, "But how white its teeth are."[3] What wisdom was this teacher imparting to his students?

Words contain energy. Positive words contain positive energy and negative words contain negative energy. How we describe ourselves, others, and our experiences, has an impact both on how we feel and how the people around us feel in our company.

Rebbe Yechiel of Alexander taught that when a person is sick, he should not say, "I am ill" but rather, "I need to be healthy."

We can choose words which energize, empower, and inspire, or we

---

1. *Pesachim*, 3a
2. *Bereishis*, 7:2
3. *Chovos HaLevavos*, Shaar Hakniah

can use words which leave us and those around us feeling down. When we are more aware of the impact of our words, we will choose them more consciously and more constructively. Using a more positive vocabulary goes a long way in elevating the quality of our lives and the quality of our interactions with others. As King Solomon expressed, "Life and death are dependent upon the quality of our speech."[4]

Reflection

What words do I commonly use to describe my life experiences?

_____
_____
_____
_____

What impact does my choice of vocabulary have on me?

_____
_____
_____
_____

How can I use language more effectively?

_____
_____
_____
_____

4. *Mishlei*, 18:20

ATTENTION

The Baal Shem Tov taught that wherever our thoughts go, there we are. Our quality of life is largely dependent upon what we choose to focus on. Oftentimes, this choice is never made. Rather, we allow our minds to go wherever they may. If we think about this tendency, it explains a lot.

When we focus on thoughts of gratitude, or are inspired by someone's example, our focus carries with it a positive emotional quality. When we aim our attention at what we dislike in others or on various annoyances in our lives, this focus brings with it a very different emotional response. For example, people who spend a lot of time focused on thoughts of inadequacy generally feel pretty down.

Considering how affected we are by what we focus on, it is amazing that we do not bring more consciousness to where we place our attention. It is possible to get stuck in thoughts which make us feel sick and simply allow ourselves to stay there. Fortunately, awareness itself can be the first step toward doing things differently.

Our minds work associatively. When our minds come to rest on something, our thoughts naturally jump to similar, related things, hopping from one related focus to another. Our quality of association is very personal and depends very much on the nature of our minds and our life experiences. By choosing what we focus on more consciously, we likewise impact the associative stream which follows.

A man once approached Rabbi E. E. Dessler and asked the following question: "Isn't the teaching of our Sages regarding the blue thread of the tzitzis a little farfetched? They say that the blue of the thread reminds us of the blue of the sea, and the blue of the sea reminds us of the blue of the sky, and the blue of the sky reminds us of Hashem's throne of glory?"

Rabbi Dessler countered, "And the law that a man should not pray opposite the colored garment of a woman (because that will lead him to think of a woman's body and this will lead him to other thoughts) – that you do understand. Why is it that when it comes to this matter, the association is clear to you, but not when it comes to the other?!"

Awareness of what we focus on, and the content of our associative thinking, gives us the freedom to evaluate and perhaps change our thought patterns. It allows us to choose what to give attention to and what not to. In doing so, we mold our minds and our emotional experience in a way which serves us to a much greater degree than does habit alone.

Reflection

What are the things I spend a lot of time thinking about?

_____
_____
_____
_____

How does focusing on these things impact me?

_____
_____
_____
_____

What would be helpful to give more attention to?

_____
_____
_____
_____

What would be helpful to give less attention to?

_____
_____
_____
_____

GRATITUDE

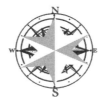

Thinking grateful thoughts has been shown to be emotionally uplifting. This is interesting considering how difficult it can be to surrender to the reality that we need others. Given the choice, we might very well choose to never be in a position which would require us to be grateful. So, why is it that feeling grateful feels good?

Part of it is that being alone is painful. Feeling one's separateness from others can hurt in the most excruciating way. In fact, isolation is a form of punishment used quite frequently by those in the punishing business. A piece of the pleasure in gratitude is feeling connected to something or someone beyond ourselves who cared enough to give us something of value.

Beyond this, humility is inherent in gratitude. There is an awareness of blessing, of getting more than we may have deserved, and appreciating the kindness received. There is an insight into one's limitations, and the goodness of others, that humbles and uplifts at the same time.

Leah was one of Jacob's four wives. The four wives of Jacob knew that he was destined to have twelve sons who would be the progenitors of the Jewish Nation. With everything else being equal, each wife should bring forth three of these future leaders. When Leah gave birth to her fourth son, she named him Judah. Judah means thanksgiving. Leah wanted to express her heartfelt gratitude to G-d for "having received more than her share."[1]

In Hebrew, the root form of the word "admit" and of the word "thanks" are the same – "modeh." This is indicative of a connection

1. Rashi, *Bereishis*, 29:35

98

between admission and gratitude[2] – When we are grateful to another, there is an admission of needing them, of not being able to get to the same place without them.

The struggle between wanting to be independent and, at the same time, needing others, is a tough one. Part of us wants to believe that we can do it all alone. And at the same time, life reminds us, again and again, that man is not an island. In order to survive and thrive, we need others. This can be hard to accept.

Paradoxically, when we allow ourselves to appreciate what we have because of others, overcoming the pull to take credit where it is not due, we experience a surge of positive energy. And when we take what we have for granted, attributing every success to ourselves, we can feel a bit hollow. Something inside us is keeping score and letting us know when our attitudes are consistent with an untold truth.

Practicing gratitude is a connecting experience. It connects us to others and to the goodness they have brought into our lives. By cultivating the mindset of gratitude, we deepen our ability to appreciate what we have and whom we have it from.

Two merchants were on their way to travel abroad for business. On the way to their ship, one of the merchants injured his foot badly on a splinter and was unable to continue. He started cursing and blaspheming.

A while later, he heard that his friend's ship had sunk at sea. He started thanking and praising G-d. As the verse says, "I thank you G-d for afflicting me . . ."[3]

Reflection

How often do I experience feelings of gratitude?

_____

_____

_____

_____

2. *Pachad Yitzchak*, Chanukah 2:2
3. *Niddah*, 31a

What are some things I could be grateful for?

_____

_____

_____

_____

Who are some people I could feel grateful toward and why?

_____

_____

_____

_____

RECIPROCITY

All ten plagues were brought upon the Egyptians by Moses except for three: Blood, Frogs, and Lice. What was different about these?

When Moses was an infant, he was placed in a basket in the Nile and was not harmed. And later, when he killed an Egyptian who was beating a fellow Jew, he hid the Egyptian in the sand. Moses said, "How can I strike the Nile, turning it into blood?[1] Is it right that one who drank from a well should throw a stone into it?"[2] So too, when it came to striking the sand and turning it into lice, Moses refrained as well.

Similarly, the Torah commands us to accept Egyptian converts because they provided a haven for us in our time of need.[3] And what about the fact that they also subjugated our nation and killed our children?! – Even so.

This law is difficult to understand. How can the Torah tell us not to reject those who caused us so much suffering and accept them into our nation? The Maharal (Rabbi Judah Loeb of Prague) explains that not reciprocating kindness is cruelty. Inasmuch as we were sojourners in their land and they did not distance us, so too, it would be wrong for us to distance them.[4] To do otherwise would be a lack of integrity.

Moses was the leader of the entire Jewish nation. One of the primary requirements of such leadership is sensitivity toward others. Part of what being sensitive to others involves is appreciating what we have received from others. If Moses had allowed his sensitivity to become dulled by showing a lack of appreciation, even to inanimate objects, this

1. *Shemos Rabbah*, 20:1
2. *Bava Kamma*, 92b
3. *Devarim*, 32:8
4. Maharal, *Chidushei Agados*, Bava Kama, 92b

would have lessened his ability to be sensitive to people as well. As a result, when it came time to bring plagues upon the Nile and the earth, Moses refrained from striking them.

Reflection

Whom have I benefited from?

_____

_____

_____

_____

How have I recognized the benefit which I have received?

_____

_____

_____

_____

How could I better recognize the benefit I have received?

_____

_____

_____

_____

PERSONAL LEADERSHIP

Moses felt a deep personal responsibility to the Jewish people and was concerned about who would lead them after his passing. He said to G-d, "Let G-d, the G-d of spirits, appoint a man over the assembly . . ." Why did Moses refer to G-d, in this request, as the "G-d of spirits"?[1]

Moses said to G-d, "Before You is revealed the mind of each and every person. And no mind is like any other. Appoint over them a leader who will bear each and every person according to whom they are."[2] G-d replied that Moses' successor will be Joshua, "A man of spirit." "Just as you asked, a person who is capable of meeting each and every individual according to whom they are."[3]

This ability to see each person as they are was a necessary component of being a prophet and a leader of Israel. Aside from the sensitivity this entails, and which is a value in itself, there is a further benefit in being able to instruct each person in their life mission according to the root of their soul and the nature of their body. The greatest service any leader can ever do for his people is to help them realize who they are. Unfortunately, when prophecy ended, so did our access to this kind of leadership.

Despite the lack of prophecy, we still have recourse to the divine spirit (Ruach Hakodesh) to lead us in finding our path. The divine spirit is like a sixth sense, rooted in the forces of holiness, with which a person can know things which are above and beyond the perception of the five senses. Despite this quality being less foolproof than prophecy, if

1. Rashi, *Bamidbar*, 27:16
2. Ibid.
3. Rashi, Bamidbar, 27:18

we refine ourselves sufficiently, we can hear its calling, and intuit the direction we need to go in.

Similarly, the Talmud teaches that even if we are not prophets, we are the sons of prophets.[4] This means that we possess an inner sense of who we are, and what we need to do, which comes from a higher place,[5] transcending reason. If we sensitize ourselves to this inner quality, it can guide us on the path we need to travel.

It may be beyond us to know the mind of each and every person we encounter, but we can at least come to know our own mind. By refining our character and developing sensitivity to our inner spirit, we can tune in to a deeper frequency and navigate our lives accordingly. In doing so, we fulfill our primary responsibility to G-d and to ourselves – to realize who we are.

Reflection

How would I describe my mind?

_____

_____

_____

_____

What path am I on?

_____

_____

_____

_____

What would help me to become more sensitive to my inner spirit?

_____

_____

_____

_____

4. *Pesachim*, 66a
5. Rav Tzaddok HaKohen, *Resisei Layla*, Os cheis

EXTERNALIZATION

In order to realize our potential, we need to consider what type of mind-set will be most effective in getting us there. The Shem MiShmuel, a profound Chassidic text,[1] reveals a deep insight into the outlook of a growing person, in the author's discussion of the core difference between Jacob and Esau. He teaches that by being aware of the attitude of Esau and emulating the approach of Jacob, we can reach much greater heights.

The root form of the name Esau, "asah," means something which is made; complete. The numeric value, or gematria[2] of the name Esau (376), is the same as the word "Shalom" (376), whose meaning is both "peace" and "completion." Esau is known as a person who was very comfortable with bloodshed. What connection could there be between the person, Esau, and the concepts of peace and completion?

Esau saw himself as being complete. In the eyes of others, he needed a lot of work, but in his own eyes, he was at peace with who he was. As far as he was concerned, he had arrived at where he needed to be.

When Jacob received the blessings of the firstborn from their father, Isaac, Esau was furious. But he saw the problem as being outside himself, in Jacob, and not in his own decision to sell the rights of the firstborn to Jacob for a bowl of lentil soup. Instead of looking at his own actions and owning up to them, he blames Jacob and decides to kill him. If he is perfect, then Jacob must be the problem. Kill Jacob and the problem will be solved.

---

1. *Shem MiShmuel*, Toldos, 5672
2. In Hebrew, each letter has a numeric value, and the *gematria* of a word is the sum of the letters in it. Our Sages say that words with the same gematria have a connection (Rashi, *Pirkei Avos*, 3:18; Rashi, *Daniel*, 8:14).

When Esau's parents are unhappy with his wives from Canaan, instead of separating from them, he simply gets another wife, from Ishmael's family. What is already under his roof is fine. There is no need to change anything. If he needs a wife with better lineage, no problem; he will simply add on to what he already has.

Jacob's life stands in stark contrast to that of Esau. Even when he earns the spiritual level to be called "Israel" – one who has struggled with angels and men and been victorious – he is still also referred to as Jacob, which refers to him as grabbing onto the heel (of Esau) at birth. No matter how much Jacob grows and develops, he continues to see himself as only grabbing onto the heel, standing at the bottom with still so far to reach.

The Chiddushei HaRim[3] was learning in the house of study. Every few minutes he would hear something bang against the side of the building from outside. He got up to see what it was and saw his grandson, who would later become the famous Sfas Emes (Chassidic leader and eminent scholar who led the Chassidim of Gur), playing a game with a few friends. He stood to watch for a while.

The boys would run up a long piece of wood which was steeply balanced against the side of the building, and try to get to the top of the ramp and slap the wall. He noticed that all the boys, with the exception of his grandson, would fall off at some point before the top, while his grandson was able to make it to the top each turn and hit the side of the building.

The Chiddushei HaRim asked his grandson, how was it that he was able to get to the top while all the other boys fell off before then? The future Sfas Emes answered that it is really quite simple. When all the other boys run up, at some point they look down, and see how high up they are, and fall down. When I run up, I only look upwards, and therefore am able to reach the top and hit the wall without falling.

Torah scholars are referred to as Talmidei Chachamim (students of the wise). So long as a Torah scholar sees himself as a student, needing to learn more Torah, he is considered a wise person. Whereas, one who considers himself to already be a wise person, and feels no need to learn any more, is neither a wise person, nor a student of wisdom.[4]

Constant striving for growth only exists in one who believes that

3. Rabbi Yitzchak Meir Alter (1799–1866) was the founder of the Chassidic dynasty of Ger, and one of the preeminent Torah scholars of his time. He is known by the name of his works on the Torah, titled *Chiddushei Harim*.
4. *Yismach Moshe*, Toldos

there is room for growth. Only one who possesses the strength to look within, and take responsibility for what is not complete, can reach a greater level of completion. This attitude personified Jacob, who fought an angelic being and won, and still saw himself as only grabbing on to the heel.

Reflection

How often do I find myself blaming others for what is unsatisfactory in my life?

_____

_____

_____

_____

When something goes wrong, how much responsibility do I take?

_____

_____

_____

_____

In which areas of my life do I feel that I have room for growth?

_____

_____

_____

_____

What are some things I can do to further this growth?

_____

_____

_____

_____

PERSONAL RESPONSIBILITY

Taking responsibility for what we could have done better has been a challenge since Adam. Adam ate from the Tree of Knowledge, acting against the commandment of G-d not to eat it. Upon being confronted with his transgression, what does he say?

It was not my fault!

Whose fault was it?

"The Woman You gave to me – she gave to me from the tree . . ."[1] It was her fault because she gave it to me. And it was Your fault, because You are the One who put her in my life.

King Saul sinned by not completely destroying all remembrance of the nation of Amalek, including the sheep and cattle, as commanded by the prophet Samuel. He said to Samuel in his defense, "I sinned because I was afraid of the nation and I listened to their voice."[2] He also used an excuse to avoid taking responsibility.

In contrast, when King David was rebuked by Nathan the prophet for the episode with Bat Sheva and Uriah the Hittite, he replied with two words, "I have sinned to G-d."[3] No cover up. No excuses. Complete acceptance of personal responsibility.

Likewise, when Judah, David's great-grandfather, realized that he had wronged Tamar, his daughter-in-law, he did not look for excuses or rationalizations. He owned up to his culpability, and stated simply, "She is more righteous than I."[4] This was despite the cost of severe personal embarrassment.

1. *Bereishis*, 3:12
2. *Shmuel I*, 15:24
3. *Shmuel II*, 12:13
4. *Bereishis*, 28:36

It is no wonder that G-d chose this family for royalty and leadership of His people. They were able to own up to their mistakes and take the appropriate actions when necessary. This is an absolute standard that G-d requires of the leaders of his people.

It is easy to fall into the trap of blaming others when we falter. All the more so when the consequences of our mistakes are serious. It takes immense personal courage to be able to accept responsibility for our wrongdoing and not shift the blame onto others.

No one likes to look bad. No one likes to be humbled by their own fallibility. Ironically, though, it is the ability of a person to accept responsibility for their own wrongdoing which frees them to rise above the fault and address it. If we believe that it was in our power to have done differently and we erred, we will also believe that we can choose better in the future, and do so.

Whereas, if we get caught up blaming others for what happens in our lives, we are saying that we are powerless against the forces around us. We are victims, unable to take the reins of our own lives. Basically, we are stuck.

It was said of Elazar ben Durdai that there was no prostitute in the world whom he did not sleep with. Once, he heard of a certain woman in a far-off island who took a pouch full of dinarim coins as her wages.

He took a pouch of money and went to find her, crossing over seven rivers. While they were together, she passed wind. She said, "Just like this wind will not return to the place it came from, so too, Elazar ben Durdai will not be accepted back in repentance."

Her words pierced his heart. He went and sat between two mountains and valleys. He said: Mountains and valleys, please pray for compassion upon me.

They responded: Before we ask for compassion upon you, we need to ask for compassion upon ourselves.

He said: Heavens and Earth, pray for compassion upon me.

They answered: Before we ask for compassion upon you, we need to ask for compassion upon ourselves.

He said: Stars and constellations pray for compassion upon me.

They answered: Before we ask for compassion upon you we need to ask for ourselves.

He finally realized: The matter rests on me alone.

He placed his head between his knees and cried bitterly until his soul left him. A heavenly voice went forth: Rebbe Elazar ben Durdai is invited to life in the eternal world.

Rebbie Yehuda cried when he heard this. He said, "There are those who acquire their world in a number of years and there are those who acquire it in a moment.[5] How great is the potential of a single moment for affecting positive change.

What was Elazar ben Durdai doing, asking all the different forces in the world to pray for him?

He really wanted to change. But he did not believe that he could do it himself. He hoped that by enlisting the help of great forces – mountains, valleys, the heavens and the earth, the stars and the constellations – then he could move forward.

Only once he realized that it depended upon him alone to help himself, was he able to take personal responsibility for his spiritual state. At that moment he turned to G-d with all his heart and soul. In doing so, he was able to elevate the content of his entire being, returning to G-d in complete repentance. He succeeded to such an extent that he was called "Rebbe" (a master and teacher) by the heavenly voice, meriting a portion in the world to come.

Reflection

What do I gain by blaming others?

_____

_____

What do I lose by doing so?

_____

_____

What do I gain by assuming greater responsibility?

_____

_____

Where in my life can I take greater personal responsibility?

_____

_____

5. *Avodah Zarah*, 17a

MAKING ROOM

Rabbi Menachem Mendel of Kotzk once asked a student, "Where is G-d?"

The student replied, "Why, He is everywhere."

The Rabbi replied, "No. He is wherever you let Him in."

One of the deepest human drives is to be independent.[1] We like to feel that we are masters of our own destiny. We can plan, set goals, and theoretically accomplish anything we put our minds to. And when we succeed, it is very tempting to consider ourselves "self-made."

Really, this perspective is half true. But not the half we might think. When it comes to spirituality, each of us has the opportunity to make of ourselves what we will. We have the power and the choice to develop our character, or not to. In the realm of physicality, however, despite the appearance that things are under our control and dependent upon our abilities, success is dependent upon the will of G-d.

If we choose to, we can see that "He is the One Who gives you strength."[2] Onkelos the convert (in his translation of the above verse) comments, "He is the One Who gives you insight as to how to acquire wealth." Onkelos is teaching us that even the ideas we have about becoming prosperous come from above.

Let us consider our own lives for a moment. We may notice that it has not necessarily been our own brilliance or diligence which has fathered whatever fortune we may enjoy. How many times have we put our hopes and aspirations in one direction only to be disappointed? And at the

---

1. *Michtav MeEliyahu*, vol. 4, pp. 27–28
2. *Devarim*, 8:18

same time, how often has some overlooked and unforeseen possibility ended up bringing success.

When we think we have it all figured out, we are in the most trouble.[3] G-d responds measure for measure. He says, "Go ahead. Let us see how well you do on your own." Looking at our own lives, this experience may also be familiar.

Rabbi Shlomo Freifeld, zt"l, illustrated this point with a personal story. He tells of someone he knew from his days in yeshiva who was incredibly talented and put-together. Every plan this person made was meticulously organized. Each eventuality and how to deal with it was thought out beforehand. There was a plan B, and if that did not work, a plan C. And yet, every venture this person touched failed, again and again.

In contrast, he told of how he started the yeshiva, Sh'or Yoshuv. He had no idea how things would come together, or how the bills would get paid week to week. And yet, thank G-d, the yeshiva survived and thrived. Seemingly, he remarked, the results should be otherwise.

Rabbi Freifeld explained that he had no idea how things were going to work out and was constantly turning to G-d. He left plenty of room for G-d, and G-d responded in kind. This other person had everything figured out already. He did not leave any room for G-d. As a result, whatever he touched failed.

As important as plans and goals are, it is no less important to leave room for G-d. To be a successful person, it is not enough to be bright or hardworking. We also need to realize where our success ultimately comes from. In doing so, we can place our confidence where it belongs and invite G-d's blessing into our lives.

Reflection

Where do I allow room for G-d in my life?

_____

_____

_____

_____

3. *Chovos HaLevavos*, Shaar HaBitachon, chap. 3

What is challenging about leaving room for G-d?

_____

_____

_____

_____

What are some ways I can successfully address these challenges?

_____

_____

_____

_____

IN PROCESS

Before G-d created this world, He engaged in a process of building worlds and destroying them, finally creating our world.[1] If G-d had wanted to, He could have created a world any way He desired from the very beginning. What need was there to build and destroy other worlds first?

Life in this world is intended as a purifying process.[2] The nature of an existence that itself is a process is, appropriately, created through a process. This quality is conveyed in the building of worlds and destroying of them prior to creating this world.

There is another facet to this. Our journey here is about choices and challenges. This is necessary in order for the intended refinement that the world was created for to take place.

When we look at the multitude of elements and objects that exist, providing just the right setting for all the challenges of the past, present, and future, we can appreciate the complexity inherent in this reality. Such a multilayered complexity is borne out from layer upon layer of existence, each built upon the other. This layering is a further dimension of the building and destroying of worlds before our own.

Getting it right is not about perfection. It is about process. Life is a process of building and of coming apart. It is a process which consists of stronger and weaker parts. It is a process of learning from what has been, for better and for worse, and using those pieces to construct a stronger future.

---

1. *Bereishis Rabbah*, 3:7
2. *Igra D'Kallah*, 87b

Reflection

What have been some stages in my process?

_____

_____

_____

_____

What lessons have these different stages taught me?

_____

_____

_____

_____

How can I use the parts of my life which have come apart to make me stronger?

_____

_____

_____

_____

BALANCE

Before we come into this world we are administered an oath: Be a tzaddik [a righteous person] and not a rasha [wicked person]. And even if the entire world tells you that you are a tzaddik, you should be in your own eyes a rasha.[1]

What meaning does an oath before birth have? And aside from this difficulty, this seems to contradict what our Sages taught in Ethics of our Fathers, that we should *not* consider ourselves to be a rasha. And if we were to see ourselves as a rasha, we would feel downcast and dejected and not be able to serve G-d with joy and gladness of heart. On the other hand, if we lack any seriousness of mood, we can become light-headed and frivolous. (Tanya, Ch. 1)

The Baal HaTanya, Rabbi Shneur Zalman of Liadi, one of the foremost Chassidic thinkers, began his monumental work, the Tanya, by setting forth the parameters of spiritual balance. If the entire world is telling us how great we are, the way to keep our footing is by going to the opposite extreme (Maimonides gives this instruction as well in the Laws of Deos[2]). At the same time, we have to keep in mind that being joyful is a basic condition for being able to serve G-d properly. If our self-critique comes at the expense of gladness of heart, we need to take a step back toward happiness. But do not step too far, because the opposite extreme is likewise undesirable.

How do we know, how do we sense, whether or not we have lost our balance? Apparently, there is some innate knowing that we possess,

1. *Niddah*, 30b
2. *Mishneh Torah*, Hilchos Deos, chap. 1, Halachos 3–4

which alerts us as to where we are up to inside. Where does this come from?

It comes from this oath we took before we entered the world. This pre-birth knowing stays with us and responds to how we live our lives. When we are true to its content, we feel joy. When we are not, we feel friction.

Rabbi Bunim of Peshischa had a student named Reb Shaul. Reb Shaul was a successful businessman. Every year he would travel to Leipzig to acquire merchandise. One year, in Leipzig, there was another merchant who had borrowed a lot of money with which he hoped to purchase merchandise. On the day of the sale in Leipzig, this merchant found that his wallet was missing and he was in great sorrow. Reb Shaul heard of this man's loss and made up his mind to help him.

Before the sale was over, Reb Shaul invited all the merchants to a feast. When the feast was ending and everybody was in a good mood, having enjoyed a nice amount of wine, Reb Shaul got up and addressed the assembled:

"My dear friends, such-and-such happened to our compatriot who comes here each year. This year he was robbed of all his money and he is unable to purchase merchandise, aside from being severely in debt. We are all going to be on our way home, joyful in what we have acquired, while at the same time, our friend cannot face going home. Therefore, I have an idea. We are one hundred strong. Let each of us give a portion, and between us, we will return to this man his loss."

Everyone respected Reb Shaul and agreed to give a part. Reb Shaul turned to the merchant who had been robbed and said to him, "You are also a merchant, like us, and should also give a portion." This merchant understandably agreed and gave his part as well. He took the money which had been collected and went home joyfully like the others.

Reb Shaul went home as well. On the way home from Leipzig, when he passed by Peshischa, Reb Shaul would always stop there and spend time with his Rabbi. As Reb Shaul arrived, Rabbi Bunim came out and greeted him, saying, "Reb Shaul, your work was nice, but you should have given the merchant all of the money, and not taken a portion from him. When it comes to charity, we don't play games."

Rabbi Bunim was surely happy with Reb Shaul for how he had helped his fellow Jew in need. But, he was also aware that it was easy for his student to feel a bit proud of himself on account of what he had done. To restore a healthy balance, he minimized in Reb Shaul's eyes the immensity of his act of kindness.

Reflection

Do I see myself more often as a tzaddik or a rasha?

_____

_____

_____

_____

How does this affect me?

_____

_____

_____

_____

What can I do to achieve greater balance?

_____

_____

_____

_____

PARTS

Rebbe Yehuda taught: "What is the straight path that a man should choose? Whatever is beautiful to the one who does it, and beautiful from the perspective of others."[1]

Why does Rebbe Yehuda add the piece about being beautiful in the eyes of others? If it is good in the eyes of the person doing it, who cares what other people think?[2]

There are a number of things that are intrinsically good. A person does them and they are beautiful to him. Just, when another person sees him, it can be cause for denigration. An example of this is when Rabbi Eliezer was wearing clothes indicative of mourning over the loss of the Holy Temple in the marketplace. Being that sensitive to such a great loss is a level. But from the vantage point of others who only see the outside, it looks like he is putting on airs.

If a path seems right in one's eyes but in the eyes of others it arouses suspicions, one should be wary. There is a need to address both the eyes of G-d and the eyes of men (this does not mean, however, to choose a life path based on people-pleasing). For example, a Torah scholar has a weighty responsibility not to do things which seem inappropriate because of how it reflects on the Torah.

The entire concept of the attribute "Tiferes," beauty, relates to the perception of the beholder, and not the one being beheld, as the saying goes, "beauty is in the eyes of the beholder." If that is the case, how does the statement, "Beautiful to the one doing it, but not beautiful in the

---

1. *Pirkei Avos*, chap. 2, Mishna 1
2. Maharal, *Derech Chaim*

eyes of the beholder," make any sense?[3]

Man is comprised of different parts. As a result, it is possible to use the term "and beautiful to the one doing it" referring even to the relationship between the person and himself, given the different parts within him.[4] Our parts can either seem beautiful to one another or not, depending upon how well they fit together.

Rabbi Hutner articulated this concept as follows: "Since man is a complex being, made up of many worlds, and the soul of man branches forth living in a number of worlds, within man there will be a place for coexistent relationships between one world and another."[5]

Human experience testifies to this inner complexity. For example, a parent marries off a child. On the one hand, they may be very happy that their child is moving forward in a meaningful relationship. On the other hand, there can be sadness at the thought of the child leaving home and the relationship changing. At the same time, there might be worry about how they are going to pay for the wedding or marry off their other children. And at the same time, there may be hopeful anticipation of grandchildren in the future.

Many life experiences evoke a host of different thoughts and emotions. It is no wonder that we feel ambivalent sometimes. A variety of different emotions converging upon us, all at once, can be confusing.

By allowing all of our parts to be heard and appropriately addressed, rather than highlighting some and ignoring others, it is possible to touch an inner point of unity which lies beneath all of our different facets. There is a deeper place from which all of our parts stem forth and which rises to the surface when we are true to our selves. By accepting and addressing our totality, in all its varied parts, we give ourselves the necessary space to be who we really are.

3. Rav Yehoshua Hartman in his comments on the Maharal, *Derech HaChaim*
4. Rabbi Hartman quoting Rav Yonasan David, *Derech HaChaim*, note 11.
5. *Pachad Yitzchak* Sefer Hazikaron, p. 350

Reflection

What path is beautiful to me?

_____

_____

_____

_____

How does it seem in the eyes of others?

_____

_____

_____

_____

What are some of my parts?

_____

_____

_____

_____

Have I disowned any of my parts?

_____

_____

_____

_____

How does this impact me?

_____

_____

_____

_____

IMITATION

"Imitation is the highest form of flattery." This may soften the annoyance of someone being imitated. But what price is the imitator paying for his compliment?

Jacob, at the end of his life, criticizes his sons Simeon and Levi. He admonishes them that stolen weapons are in their hands.[1] Jacob is referring to when Simeon and Levi, following the abduction of their sister Dina by Shechem, took sword in hand and wiped out the entire city of Shechem. He was telling them, "You stole the attribute of Esau!"

Esau's inheritance is "by the sword you shall live" – not yours! By taking hold of his attribute, you have lost your own. You have become inauthentic, disconnected from who you really are.[2]

We cannot know G-d if we do not know who we are.[3] Knowledge of self serves as a basis for all further wisdom. If this is missing, what is there?

Rabbi Yerucham Levovitz recounts that he once met a man, and as they were talking, he noticed that the man's gestures and movements were exactly like those of someone else he knew. He asked the man if he knew the person that he reminded him of. The man answered, "Of course! He and I are like brothers. We are extremely close."

Rabbi Levovitz was amazed. He reflected how it is possible for a person to possess qualities which are not their own. It is even possible for someone to be "completely borrowed" from others, lacking even the smallest personal input; completely stolen.[4]

1. *Bereishis*, 49:5
2. *Daas Torah*, Vayechi
3. *Ibn Ezra*, Shemos 31:18
4. *Daas Torah*, Vayechi

It is worthwhile considering which parts of us are truly are own. We unconsciously absorb qualities and nuances from the people around us. By checking with ourselves what is really ours and what is not, we can live a life which is authentically our own.

Reflection

Which of my parts may be borrowed?

_____

_____

_____

_____

Which of my parts are authentically mine?

_____

_____

_____

_____

What would help me to be more genuine?

_____

_____

_____

_____

THE FOUR ELEMENTS

Gaining some clarity into the nature of our strengths and our weaknesses can be challenging. We did not come with an instruction book listing exactly who we are, what our spiritual makeup is, and what we should do with our life (although that might have been helpful). It would be useful to have some guidelines with which to recognize our greatest opportunities for growth.

Fortunately, Rabbi Chaim Vital, the prime disciple of the Arizal (the foremost latter kabbalist), provided such guidelines.[1] He taught that there are four spiritual elements which lie at the root of all of our positive and negative traits: Fire, Water, Wind, and Earth. Each of us is made up of a combination of all of these elements. At the same time, each of us is unique in the mixture and composition of the specific elements which constitute who we are.

Each of these spiritual forces is associated with specific positive and negative character traits. On the negative side, Fire is associated with arrogance and anger. A person who is arrogant naturally becomes angry at whoever acts contrary to their wishes. If the person was humble, and had a healthy estimation of who he really was, he would not get angry at all. There are three offshoots of this root: (1) Being annoyed in one's heart, because if not for arrogance, one would not be so annoyed. (2) Desiring to rule over others and to be given honors; to elevate one's standing above others. (3) Hating others – because in some way, they are greater; also a natural extension of arrogance.

The element of Wind is associated with empty words. It is speech without any value on either a physical or a spiritual plane. This root has

---

1. *Shaarei Kedusha*, chaps. 1, 2

four offshoots: (1) Flattery, (2) Lies, (3) Speaking derogatorily of others, (4) Singing one's own praises in front of others to gain status.

The element of Water is associated with desiring physical pleasure, as it is water which causes all types of physical pleasures to grow. Its offshoots are two: (1) Coveting another's money, wife, or possessions in order to enjoy them for oneself. (2) Being jealous of another who possesses more than you do in some regard.

The element of Earth is associated with being emotionally down. It has one offshoot: Laziness. Because a person is upset at not having acquired more earthly goods or has had to deal with some suffering, he is not able to enjoy anything he possesses. He lives in perpetual dissatisfaction, unmotivated to advance himself spiritually.

These expressions of the four elements represent the main categories of negativity which a person can fall prey to. On the positive side, we have the potential to achieve their opposites. Opposite the Fire of arrogance, there is humility, to the extent that a person can be so far removed from arrogance that the slightest hint of anger stemming from it does not arise within him.

Opposite the Wind of empty words, there is the ability to be silent, only using the faculty of speech for constructive purposes. Opposite the Waters of avarice, there is a spiritual contentment, above the pull of vices and excess. Opposite the heaviness of Earth, there is joyfulness of heart, satisfied that whatever Hashem does is for the good, enlivened to pursue a higher path.

Each of us will connect more to some of these strengths and weaknesses than others. Take note which areas resonate more strongly. And remember, as Rabbi Tzaddok HaKohen taught, our greatest areas of challenge are also our greatest spheres of potential.

Reflection

Which of the four elements do I relate to the most?

_____

_____

_____

_____

How is this element expressed in my life?

_____

_____

_____

_____

What potential for good is inherent in this force?

_____

_____

_____

_____

What are some things I can do to strengthen the positive side of this element?

_____

_____

_____

_____

THREE ROOTS

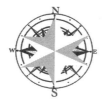

Each person is their own unique combination of elements, and at the same time, there are a few common roots that we all share.[1] Within us lie three primary energies which influence our thoughts and actions. Each of these forces is distinct in its spiritual nature as well as in its practical expression. Inside every one of us, one of these energies will be more dominant than the others.

These forces are known as Chessed (lovingkindness), Yiras Shamayim (fearing G-d), and Emes (truth):

A Chessed-oriented person looks outward. Their primary focus is on how to positively benefit others.

The Yiras-Shamayim-type person is inwardly focused. Their sights are set on self-mastery. On controlling what happens within so that nothing improper comes out. As Ethics of our Fathers teaches (4:1), "Who is the mighty one? The one who conquers their inclination."

The Emes-focused, or truth-focused person strives to walk a fine line between these two poles, careful not to tip the balance toward either extreme. He walks a middle path; neither of exaggerated kindness, nor of too eager self-critique, which can limit one's doing.

Each one of these attributes can move a person to greater development of the other two, but from a different point of motivation. One whose primary attribute is Chessed will come to kindness from a natural inner drive to benefit others. And he may be fearful, filled with concern that perhaps his kindness may fall short of what is required of him. Or he may aspire that his kindness be completely true, that the recipient receive the correct and necessary assistance.

---

1. *Michtav MeEliyahu*, vol. 2, pp. 160–161

Along the same lines, one whose primary trait is fear of Heaven will be fearful in every act, lest they come to do something improper. And, they may also come to practice kindness because of a fear that they have not acted properly without sufficiently benefiting others. In addition, this fear may also strengthen them in matters of truth, because without truth, their actions are lacking in integrity.

Similarly, when speaking of those motivated by truth, such people desire truthfulness because this quality resonates with who they are. They may be moved to kindness because of their recognition of the truth inherent in kindness. And likewise, their desire for truthfulness may bring them to a fear of being distanced from truth.

We vary from each other in the attributes we connect to the most. The quality that resonates with us most strongly is our spiritual bedrock. It is an underlying theme, which expresses itself compellingly in both our thoughts and our actions.

The first step in our inner work is to recognize and reveal our primary trait; to open it up and develop it fully, according to the Torah's guidelines; to be true to it.

The next step is to use our primary trait as a doorway through which to develop the other traits. By knowing our primary trait, we can motivate ourselves effectively as to how to develop the other qualities we possess – we have found the correct method to maximize who we are.

During the Polish revolt against Russia, Rabbi Yitzchak Isaac Yom Tov was traveling from Warsaw to Vorki to see the great Tzaddik, Rabbi Yitzchak of Vorki. Many Chassidim were traveling together with him, when they were stopped by Polish soldiers who asked the Chassidim if they had seen any Russian soldiers. The Chassidim replied that they had not, but even so, the soldiers took Rabbi Yitzchak Isaac and left.

The Chassidim stayed where they were, hoping against all hope that this holy person would be returned to them. After two hours, the soldiers brought back Rabbi Yitzchak Isaac, saying, "He is a man of truth. His countenance testifies that he would never lie."

Reflection

Which of these three traits do I feel most connected to?

_____

_____

_____

_____

How is this trait expressed in my life?

_____

_____

_____

_____

What can I do to strengthen it?

_____

_____

_____

_____

How can I use this trait as an access point through which I can develop my other traits?

_____

_____

_____

_____

LEARNING STRENGTHS

Just as there are different character strengths, so too, there are different learning strengths. The Sages disputed who should be the next head of their yeshiva. Should they choose a person with breadth of knowledge, or a person who can uproot mountains, capable of delving deeply into the topic being studied? Rav Yosef possessed breadth of knowledge, and Rabbah could uproot mountains. The Talmud concludes that the person with breadth of knowledge should preside because everyone needs the one who knows a lot.[1]

This does not mean that this was deemed a greater strength and that everyone should take the approach of Rav Yosef, focusing on amassing knowledge, somewhat at the expense of depth. It means that this is what worked for him, and when it comes to being in a position of serving the masses, this was deemed a more important qualification. But even Rav Yosef himself, in choosing how to learn, did not do so with this end in mind. He learned in the way that worked best for him.

Rav Yosef and Rabbah each understood which type of learning was right for them, and used that understanding to achieve their levels of excellence. Had they imitated each other, neither of them would have been candidates to head the yeshiva. They would have left their own strength underdeveloped and, at the same time, fallen short of the level of their friend, in his strength. That would have been a tragic waste for each of them as individuals, as well as for the nation they served, each with their own strength in wisdom.

There are three main qualities of wisdom: Chochma, Bina, and Daas.

1. *Huriyos*, 14a

Chochma is about receiving information.[2] This is naturally the first step in becoming a person of wisdom.[3] The next step is about taking what one has learned and understanding the reasons behind it, inferring and deriving one thing from another. This process of building upon what one knows is called Bina.[4] Daas is the ability to discern and weigh different things, knowing where to put one's personal dividing line.[5]

Chochma is outwardly focused, looking to take in the wisdom of others. Bina is inwardly focused, looking to deepen the wisdom one already has. Daas is a synthesis of these two forces, combining aspects of both Chochma and Bina to discern the nature and quality of different things.

In each person, all of these qualities exist and are necessary. The question is, where are we stronger, and where are we weaker? By identifying where we excel and where we struggle, we can more effectively structure our learning process, managing for where we are weak and maximizing where we are strong. In doing so, we raise our learning curve significantly.

If we are very strong in our desire and enjoyment of learning new things, excelling in Chochma, it makes sense that we will experience the greatest growth in this area and should invest in it accordingly. It is true that we need to get to a passable level in the other wisdom qualities, and to be basically competent in our areas of weakness. But, to put all of our time and energy into remediation would be a waste of potential, aside from being demoralizing.

So too, those of us who feel thrilled at taking an idea and exploring its depths, excelling in Bina, would be best served by putting a greater emphasis on this type of learning. Again, if there is a poverty of knowledge, some time needs to be invested in Chochma. But to turn that into the sole focus would be a waste of potential.

Likewise, those of us who have a strong ability for analyzing and weighing information, enjoying the process of making fine distinctions and practical applications, excel in daas. Naturally, daas requires a basic level of information, coupled with an ability to think deductively, which takes a certain level of investment. However, the overall balance should allow for maximizing strength in daas, while giving the other qualities their due without making them the primary focus.

2. Rashi, *Mishlei*, 4:7
3. *Mishlei*, 4:7
4. Rashi, ibid.
5. Talmud Yerushalmi, *Berachos*, 5:2; *Pri Tzaddik*, Trumah, 13

Reflection

In which quality of wisdom do I experience the greatest strength and enjoyment?

_____

_____

_____

_____

What are some things I can do to strengthen this quality?

_____

_____

_____

_____

Is there any area of weakness I need to manage for?

_____

_____

_____

_____

What do I need to invest in this?

_____

_____

_____

_____

ORDER

Order in mind and in life keeps us together. Order is like the knot in a string of pearls.[1] In and of itself, it has little value. But undo it, and all the pearls will fall to the ground.

There are three kinds of order.[2] The first type is order for its own sake, like the beauty of a well-arranged garden, with each item in its set place. The garden would not be nearly as beautiful if all the different plants and flowers were growing mixed together.

The second type of order is one of convenience. To save time, energy, and frustration, we place our things in specific places so that we can find them when we need to. And, when we finish using something, we are usually well served by returning it to its place, so that we can locate it in the future.

The third type of order is one of function. It is the type found in machines. It involves many parts, each performing its role, in its place, to produce the desired results. If some disconnect occurs between the parts, or the sequence of operation gets mixed up, the machine ceases to work.

This is also the type of order which lies at the heart of creation and at the core of the Jewish Nation. The goal of creation is accomplished through the collective efforts of all the individuals throughout all the generations. Each plays their part, with their varied situations, and by way of their diverse characteristics. The totality is arrived at by each component contributing what it has to offer to the whole.[3]

1. *Daas Torah,* "Bamidbar," p. 17
2. *Michtav MeEliyahu,* vol. 1, pp. 92–93
3. *Mei HaShiloach, Bamidbar,* 1:2

This type of order was also found in the encampment of the Jewish people in the desert. Their organization was precise. Each tribe camped by their flag and traveled according to a specific sequence, in an exact configuration. Camping out in another's section or traveling out of order was not an option, no less than being someone else was an option.

Each tribe possessed a distinctive quality. Judah's was leadership. Issachar's was wisdom. Zebulun's was business acumen. Reuben's was kindness.[4] Gad's was mightiness. Asher's was lighting up the darkness.[5] Dan's was meting out justice. [6] Naphtali's was swiftness.[7] Simeon's was severity.[8] Levi's was judgment.[9] Joseph's was righteousness. Benjamin's was clear light.[10] Every tribe played a different part, which was vital to the well being and success of the whole, as did the individual members of those tribes. The order they kept was a safeguard against losing sight of who they were.

With the absence of clear tribal directives, we need to find our own order. At the same time, the character themes of the different tribes represent a basic map of organizing principles, which together comprise the totality of the Jewish people. By exploring the different qualities of the tribes and identifying which one most resonates with us, we can discover what we need to focus on in developing our character. Doing so points us in the direction of gathering in our own lost tribe, so that we can return it to the nation.

When the patriarch Isaac became aware that he had given the firstborn's blessings to Jacob, and not to Esau, he became very afraid. He saw Gehinnom (purgatory) open before him. Isaac feared that he had upset the natural order of the world by conferring the portion of the firstborn on Jacob, who had been born second. Only once Isaac found out that Jacob had bought the firstborn rights from Esau was his mind put to rest. From here we see how substantial order was understood to be by one of the greatest men ever.

4. *Likutei Torah*, Vayeitzeh
5. Ramban, *Bamidbar*, 2:2
6. Rashi, Parshas Vayechi, 49:16
7. Rashi, Parshas Vayechi, 49:21
8. *Likutei Torah*, Vayeitzeh
9. *Rikanti*, Shoftim
10. *Kehillas Yaakov*, Erech B"N

Reflection

Which type(s) of order would be helpful to me?

_____

_____

_____

_____

What are some things I can do to implement this order in my life?

_____

_____

_____

_____

Which of the tribal qualities do I relate to the most?

_____

_____

_____

_____

What are some things I can do to strengthen this quality?

_____

_____

_____

_____

RECOGNIZING ONE'S PLACE

It can be challenging to recognize one's place. The Sages listed this attribute of "recognizing one's place" as one of the forty-eight attributes through which Torah wisdom is acquired.[1] This makes sense, as it is necessary to work on the level we are presently at, if we want to reach the level beyond that. Whereas, if we delude ourselves into thinking that we are on some level that we are not, we have stepped off the ladder of growth into thin air. To move forward in wisdom, or anything else, we need to find the appropriate rung and climb upwards from there.[2]

There was a young Torah scholar near the town of Apta who engaged in self-affliction to reach higher levels of spirituality. He refrained from eating meat or any other food from a living creature. He slept on the ground, and even then only slept a little, staying up most nights.

One day, he decided to visit the famous Tzaddik of Apta, known as the Ohev Yisrael. He concluded that if the Tzaddik was able to divine his great levels of holy service, he would remain with him and become one of his followers. And if the Tzaddik was unable to perceive his greatness, then he would return home and travel no more.

When he came to the Tzaddik, he found the Ohev Yisrael sitting by his table and eating lunch. The Tzaddik neither greeted him, nor honored him in any way. This young man was taken aback and started to leave. As he walked out he thought to himself, "What does this Tzaddik know anyway?"

The Ohev Yisrael sent the young man a message to wait for him to finish his lunch and then he would speak with him. When the Tzaddik

---

1. *Pirkei Avos*, chap. 6
2. Maharal, *Derech Chaim*, chap. 6, Mishna 7

finally came, he greeted the young man and invited him to take a walk with him through the garden. He showed the young man the stable where he kept his horses.

The young man was dumbfounded, and asked why he was being shown the horses. The Tzaddik replied, "These horses sleep little. When they sleep, it is upon the ground. And they never eat food which comes from a living creature. They have all different types of affliction, but in the end, they are just horses."[3]

The message found its mark and the young man became a student of the Rebbe, eventually becoming a genuinely great person. Only by being able to recognize who he was, and who he was not, was this young man able to reach what he was capable of. He had found his place.

Reflection

Where am I on the ladder of growth?

_____

_____

_____

_____

How do my actions fit where I am up to?

_____

_____

_____

_____

What are some things I can do to climb up to the next rung?

_____

_____

_____

_____

3. *Sippurei Hasidim*, Moadim, pp. 152–153

THE OTHER

Even the very greatest can err in estimating where they are up to, and where they are not. Four of the greatest Sages entered a very deep spiritual world called the Pardes.[1] Only Rebbe Akiva entered and left without harm. Ben Zoma lost his mind. Ben Azzai died. And Rebbe Elisha ben Avuyah became a heretic.[2]

Following this, Rebbe Elisha propositioned a prostitute.[3] She said to him, "Are you not the great Sage, Elisha ben Avuyah?" He replied, "No, he is 'Acher' – some other person." From then on, this errant Sage became known as "the other" – "Acher."

Rebbe Meir was a student of Rebbe Elisha ben Avuyah and continued learning from him even after he became Acher. One Sabbath, Acher was riding on a horse, and Rebbe Meir was following behind, on foot, to learn Torah from him. Acher turned to Rebbe Meir and said, "Meir, go back! I have counted by the footsteps of my horse that you have come to the limit you are allowed to travel on the Sabbath." Rebbe Meir replied, "You too should go back [from your ways]!" Acher countered, "Have I not already told you that I heard a heavenly voice saying, 'Wayward sons return, except for Acher'?"

Rebbe Meir knew about this heavenly voice and still was certain that Acher could repent. It might be harder for him than the average person because of certain things he had done, but the doors of return are never closed. He could still come back and G-d would receive him.[4]

---

1. They entered into a very deep spiritual world where they hoped to fix the damage done by the sin of Adam Harishon. See Sefer HaLikutim, Parshas Pekudei, chap. 38.
2. *Chagigah*, 14b
3. *Chagigah*, 15a
4. *Shnei Luchos HaBris*, Rosh HaShana, Teshuva Hamishis

But Acher was not open to this. The heavenly voice had proclaimed that "Acher" would not be received in repentance. As long as Elisha ben Avuyah identified him as being "Acher," someone other than himself, he would be distant from G-d.[5] Elisha saw himself as being this "other" who transgressed Sabbath and had illicit relations. In doing so, he limited himself to the possibilities that were open to such a person. This excluded the possibility of changing his ways. Had he been able to see past this image of Acher, to his true self, Elisha ben Avuyah, he would have been able to return.

How often do we identify with things which are "other" than our true selves? To be connected to who we are, and to be connected to G-d, we need to examine the picture we have of ourselves and see how real it is. There is a distinct possibility that because of varied life experiences and the influences of different people, we have bought into an identity that is limiting and not altogether accurate. By taking a second look at who we are, and are not, we can free ourselves to become who we might be.

Reflection

What are some behaviors which I identify with?

_____

_____

_____

How well do these behaviors represent my true self?

_____

_____

_____

What is the difference between those things which are truly me and those things which are not?

_____

_____

_____

5. *Akeidas Yitzchok*, Shaar 23

NAMES

If we are in touch with our essence, we will be able to detect our life's work. The verse says, "And Bezalel made the ark out of acacia wood . . ." (Exodus, 37:1).

Why does the verse credit Bezalel with making the ark, while there were a number of other craftsmen who were also involved?

Rashi explains that Bezalel gave himself over to this work above and beyond everyone else and therefore it was called by his name.

Why did Betzalel invest himself so completely in building the ark? What was different about him? And, what was the significance of it being called by his name?

In Biblical Hebrew, the gematria (numeric value) of the word for "his name" (sh'mo) is 346. The gematria of the word "will" (ratzon) is also 346. This indicates that there is an underlying connection between a person and their will.

What is a will? And what is a name?

The will is an inner force which lies at the core of our being. It has incredible power to move us,[1] and is connected to the fulfillment of our mission in the world. Each of us possesses a unique will, which is part of our essence.

A name is made up of Hebrew letters. The letters which construct our names are representative of the "lights" that make up who we are, reflecting our spiritual roots.[2] Each letter is made up of strokes of the pen to the right, to the left, and to the middle. This is sym-

---

1. *Leshem Shevo V'Achlama*, Hakdamos VeShearim, Shaar 7, chap. 3
2. *Arvei Nachal*, Parshas Pinchas

bolic of the various combinations of qualities which we consist of.[3]

A name is something which is revealed. We call a person or a thing by its name and we know who or what we are talking about. What we associate with the name of a person is what he has revealed of himself in the world.

A will is more concealed. It does not become evident until it is brought forth into actuality. If it is never expressed, as far as others are concerned, it never existed.

Betzalel felt that making the ark was a work his very existence was tied to. He gave himself to it more than anyone else did because he felt that his life force depended on it more than anyone else did. The expression of his name (the letters of "Bezalel") and all it represented was manifested in this work. For Bezalel, making the ark was a work of connecting the pieces of his inner will (ratzon = 346) and his outer name (sh'mo = 346).

In our own lives, we need to ask ourselves if there is some project or undertaking which moves us like nothing else does. If there is, this is a sure sign that we need to address this inner force (within the bounds of Jewish Law and common sense) and work to bring our vision into actuality. In this way we reveal the unique inner light which lies at the heart of our name.

Reflection

What is my name and what can I learn about myself from it?

_____

_____

What type(s) of activities do I feel drawn to?

_____

_____

What are some things I can do to move forward in these activities?

_____

_____

---

3. The primary energies of chessed, gevurah, and tiferes. Chesed to the right, gevrurah to the left, and tiferes in the middle.

INSIGHT

Before the soul (neshama) enters the body, it can see from one end of the world to the other.[1] Because the soul is not yet in the body, it exists on a higher plane. From this vantage point, physical space is not a limitation and it can therefore see from one end of the world to the other.[2]

Sometimes we may get an insight or a premonition of danger, and not be quite sure where it is coming from. The Talmud reveals that even if we do not see, our mazal[3] does.[4] What does this mean?

Our soul exists on many levels. Only the lowest part of it enters our body. This part of us, which exists on a higher plane, perceives things which are happening above. Even if our physicality prevents us from seeing the whole picture, we can still glimpse a shadow. But we have to be looking.

Nachmanides asked, "Why did G-d only choose to communicate with Abraham, before any mention is made of him doing anything extraordinary?"[5]

The Sfas Emes answered that G-d did not only choose Abraham. He was speaking to everyone. But only Abraham was listening.[6] Abraham was aware of a higher reality and was therefore open to hearing its voice.

By remembering where we come from, we too can open ourselves to something beyond the here and now. We can sense our souls, a spiritual

---

1. *Niddah*, 30b
2. Maharal, *Chiddushei Aggados*, 4, p. 153
3. The term *mazal* here refers to a part of our soul which exists in the higher worlds and is privy to communication there.
4. *Megillah*, 3a
5. *Ramban*, Lech Lecha
6. *Sfas Emes*, Lech Lecha, 5632

existence attached to the highest spiritual worlds, above and beyond any physical limitation. When we live in a way which respects this inner greatness, we too will be able to hear its call.

Reflection

What are some examples of insight or premonition that I have experienced?

_____

_____

_____

_____

How often do I experience such things?

_____

_____

_____

_____

What are some things I can do to become more open to my higher reality?

_____

_____

_____

_____

THE SEEING HEART

"As water reflects a face to a face, so too the heart of man to man."[1]

Our hearts possess great power. They can feel the love or hate of another.[2] They can feel closeness and distance in relationships.[3] And they can influence the hearts of others with their own feelings of love or hate.[4] But they can only see as far as we let them.[5]

When Jacob decided to leave the house of Lavan, he tells his wives that the heart of Lavan is not with him as it had been in the past. Jacob needed divine protection to protect him from Lavan's having discovered his desire to escape. As a result, when Lavan catches up to Jacob, he says to him, "You stole my heart" – from being able to see what was in your heart.[6]

Later, Jacob meets up with his brother, Esau, for the first time since receiving the blessings from Isaac that Esau had wanted. Esau hates him, and has every intention of carrying out his old desire to kill Jacob, bringing with him an army of four hundred men. And yet, Jacob is able to momentarily change Esau's heart toward him through sheer force of his own positive emotion.

Similarly, with Joseph in Egypt, after Benjamin has been brought down and "found guilty" of stealing Joseph's cup, Judah approaches Joseph to offer himself in place of Benjamin. Judah fills his heart with

---

1. *Mishlei*, 27:19
2. *Panim Yafos*, Bereishis, 27:44
3. *Ksav Sofer*, Bereishis, 31:20
4. *Ohr HaChaim*, Bereishis, 44:10
5. *Ohr HaChaim*, Bereishis, 42:8
6. See *Ksav Sofer*, Bereishis, 42:8

love for Joseph, even though, as far as he knows, Joseph is an Egyptian ruler. He does this in order that his words be well received.[7]

At the same time, the brothers of Joseph were unable to recognize their brother. He was standing right in front of them and none of them had any clue that this Egyptian ruler was none other than Joseph. How is that possible?

The brothers had made up their minds that their brother Joseph could not be in such a high position. Their judgment of Joseph blinded them. Had they been softer in their judgment, they would have felt a kinship with the ruler of Egypt, and have realized that it was their brother who was standing before them.[8]

To benefit from the wisdom of the heart, we need to open ourselves up to its voice. We need to be open to our feelings in order to benefit from the knowledge they have to offer us. Sometimes we may feel that certain feelings are not acceptable and as a result shut ourselves off from acknowledging their very existence. When we make a habit of not acknowledging our inner experience we do ourselves a great disservice.

By developing a position of greater openness, we can get in touch with more of ourselves. This allows us to connect more deeply to who we are, as well as to others. As simple as it sounds, we need to give ourselves permission to feel and reflect on our feelings, before we judge them and cut them off.

Reflection

What are some examples of how my feelings toward others impacts how others feel toward me?

_____

_____

_____

How can I influence others positively with my heart?

_____

_____

_____

7. *Ohr HaChaim*, Bereishis, 42:8
8. *Ohr HaChaim*, Bereishis, 42:8

What are some examples of how I ignore what I am experiencing?

_____

_____

_____

_____

What would help me to become more aware of my inner experience?

_____

_____

_____

_____

JUDGING

Our Sages taught in Ethics of our Fathers not to judge our fellow man until we have walked in his shoes.[1] On the other hand, they also taught that when we judge, we should do so favorably.[2] To judge or not to judge, that is the question.

Invariably, when we meet someone, we size them up. Part of this sizing up involves some judging of the other person based upon our beliefs and perspectives, and how the person in the defendant's box measures up to these. The first teaching, "do not judge," is instructing us to take a step back and rein in this tendency to judge others. Realize that we are not in a position to judge accurately. We could not possibly know and understand all that would be necessary to fully understand the person in front of us.

The second teaching is speaking to us when we are presented with a situation which can be viewed in more than one way. Our first-glance interpretation is likely to be negative. In that case, try to find a favorable way to evaluate the other person. Get creative if need be.

What is all this judgment about?

The Path of the Just[3] teaches[4] that it is part of human nature to want to place ourselves above others. We naturally compare ourselves to others and are biased when it comes to making this comparison. When we allow ourselves the smallness of cutting someone else down, it generally

---

1. *Pirkei Avos*, 2:4
2. Vayikra 19:15, *Rav O. Bartenura*
3. A famous ethical work by the great kabbalist Rabbi Moshe Chaim Luzatto. In Hebrew, known as *Mesillas Yesharim*.
4. *Mesillas Yesharim*, chap. 4

has a lot more to do with our own shortcomings than it does with the person we are evaluating.

When it comes to "serving G-d," we also compare ourselves to others. For this reason, it is essential to distinguish between what we do out of a need to elevate ourselves above others, and that which stems from a true desire to be closer to our Creator. The former is an act of serving oneself, and the latter is an act of serving G-d.

How can we tell the difference?

If we find ourselves looking over our shoulders, hoping to be seen, or if our thoughts are self-inflating, this is a pretty good indicator of whom our "service" is about.

Someone once asked the Kotzker Rebbe, "Did our Sages not teach that a person who runs away from honor, honor runs after them?[5] Well, I have been running away from honor, but it has not run after me?!"

The Kotzker replied, "It was running after you. But when it saw you looking over your shoulder, it ran away."

When we are aware of our own stuff, we are in a much better position to realize what our judgment of others is about. If we are honest, we can see how much of it is colored by our need to see ourselves in a good light. This awareness allows us to appreciate our judgment in the proper context.

Reflection

What are some examples of how I judge others?

_____

_____

_____

_____

How favorable is my judgment?

_____

_____

_____

_____

5. *Eiruvin* 13b

What is influencing the way I see others?

_____

_____

_____

_____

What would help me to judge more favorably?

_____

_____

_____

_____

A GOOD EYE

There is a famous prayer written by the illustrious Chassidic master, Rabbi Elimelech of Lizhensk. In it, he asks G-d to help him see the positive attributes of others and not their faults.

Why should seeing others favorably, to the extent of not seeing their faults, be something to pray for? As important as it is to judge favorably, is it not also important to see others' faults, to be able to guard ourselves from them?

Rebbe Yochanan ben Zakkai[1] questioned his disciples: "What is the good path which a person should attach himself to?"[2] Rebbe Eliezer (the son of Hurkenos) answered, "A good eye."

The Maharal[3] teaches that the attribute of a good eye brings enormous benefit to the one who possesses it.[4] He explains that this quality is unique in its frequency. Every moment, a person with a good eye can look around them and see the inner wealth, beauty and majesty of others. As opposed to other attributes, which are not always possible to exercise, the person with this strength fixes their gaze on their neighbor, and in a fraction of a second, he is connected to this virtue.

The Maharal defines "a good eye" as possessing a desire for others to be in a state of goodness and completion. In contrast, someone with a "bad eye" begrudges others what they have.[5] This bad eye is destruc-

---

1. One of the foremost Sages of the Mishnaic Era
2. *Pirkei Avos*, chap. 2, Mishna 13
3. One of the foremost giants of Jewish thought, he lived about 400 years ago. (Maharal is an acronym for the name of Rabbi Judah Loeb of Prague.)
4. *Derech Chaim*, on Mishna above
5. Maharal, *Nesivos Olam*, Nesiv Ayin Tov, chap. 1

tive both to the person who possesses it, as well as to the object of their focus.

Generally speaking, the way others relate to us has a lot to do with our orientation toward them. If we see others in a positive light and relate to them accordingly, it is very likely that what we will find is positive. The same could be said of how we relate to ourselves.

A story is told of a man who was very unhappily married. He found his wife to be angry, selfish, and disrespectful of him. Subsequently, he divorced her. A few years later, she remarried and had an amazing name in the community, with people singing her praises. The man went to the rabbi of the town and asked him how it could be that when he was married to her, she was such a difficult person. And now, she is such a different person for the good.

The rabbi answered that it is really quite simple. When you were married to her, all you saw were her negative traits, and that is what you got. Her present husband sees all that is good in her, and that is what he got.

Rebbe Elimelech of Lizhensk understood how powerful an impact one's outlook on others can have, both on oneself, as well as on others. As a result, he prayed to G-d to always see what was positive in others, and not their shortcomings. Seeing others with such an eye influenced the way he related to others, as well as how others related to him.

Perhaps we should also pray to see others in a positive light. Doing so will not only affect how we feel toward people, but will also impact how they feel about us. Considering how much of our life depends on the success of our relationships, this would be a wise investment.

Reflection

Imagine what it would be like to only see the good in others and not their faults. What would that be like?

_____

_____

_____

_____

How would this impact my relationships?

_____

_____

_____

How would this impact how I feel about myself?

_____

_____

_____

_____

RESPECT

There are those who demand respect and there are those who command respect. The difference between the two is huge. Through our daily conduct, we place ourselves into one category or the other. If we want to know which category we are in, we need to look at the way we treat others.

Our Sages gave us a recipe for commanding respect. Who is the respected one? -The one who respects others.[1] Ben Zoma, who taught this message, based it on the verse, "Those who honor Me [G-d], are honored [by G-d]. The Keren Ora[2] explains that this is because honoring others is tantamount to honoring G-d. Why should this be so?

The Torah teaches us that man was created in the image of G-d.[3] This means that man was invested with such incredibly vast spirituality that he is capable of moving worlds.[4] He possesses a connection to the deepest and highest of places. Respecting someone that G-d endowed with such richness is akin to respecting the One Who invested the person with that richness.

How much more would we respect others if we remembered this? How much more would we respect ourselves if we remembered this?

It was said of Rebbe Yochanan ben Zakkai that he never failed to be the first to greet another.[5] This Tanna[6] was the mentor to some of the greatest Sages of all time. He understood, better than most, the

1. *Pirkei Avos*, 4:1
2. *Taanis*, 20b
3. *Bereishis*, 1:27
4. *Nefesh HaChaim*, Shaar 1, chaps. 1–4
5. *Berachos*, 17a
6. Sage of the Mishnaic Era

inestimable value and potential of a human being and how to bring it out. He honored them. (In Ethics of our Fathers, 2:8, we find that he recognized and highlighted the specific strengths and qualities of each of his students.)

He did not need to wait and see if he would be honored first. He was big enough that it was not a concern. G-d's honor and the honor of his fellow man were far more important.

There are so many little ways to honor each other. It is amazing how different a request feels if there is a "please" attached to it. It is remarkable how far a "thank you" can go in making someone feel recognized. A sincere "good morning" can set the tone for an entire day. Aside from the reward of giving, there is an even greater return in the person we become when we regularly honor others.

At a gathering of the Sfas Emes[7] with his Chassidim, he called to one Chassid in particular to receive some wine. This Chassid wanted to approach the Rebbe, and pushed himself over a number of other people crowded there to get closer. When the Sfas Emes noticed this, he turned toward the man with an expression of annoyance on his face. A little while later, this Chassid became ill, and he was concerned that it was because he had upset the Sfas Emes. Later on, when the man got better, he went to visit the Sfas Emes. The man said to his Rebbe, "I am afraid that because I upset you, this sickness came upon me."

The Sfas Emes replied, "Do you suspect me that I would cause any punishment to come upon a single Jew."

The Chassid, rationalizing his behavior, said, "A Jew is like a Torah scroll, and what difference does it make if one Torah scroll goes on top of another."

The Sfas Emes countered, "What is required of a Jew is to treat others with the respect due to a Torah scroll.

---

7. A renowned Chassidic leader, he was the second Rebbe of the Gur Dynasty.

Reflection

How respectfully do I treat others? (Whom do I treat more respectfully, and whom do I treat less so?)

_____

_____

_____

_____

What influences how respectfully I treat others?

_____

_____

_____

_____

What are some things I can do to treat others more respectfully?

_____

_____

_____

_____

FRIENDSHIP

Respect is a basic element in any real friendship. And still, there are different kinds of friends. Some friends are out of necessity. Some friends are out of enjoyment. And some friendships touch a much deeper place, like the bond between David and Jonathan. This friendship transcended even the kingship of the Jewish people.

King Saul, Jonathan's father, saw in David a threat to his throne. He went so far as to try and kill David himself in order to pass the throne on to his son. But Jonathan, in his love of David, stood in the way. He warned David and helped him to escape, all the while knowing that his loyalty meant that David would be the next king and not him.[1]

Why was Jonathan willing to make such a sacrifice?

A love of essence, like the love of one's very soul, powerful beyond all other loves, existed between him and David. There was a mutual recognition of exquisite beauty and innate goodness, of two majestic souls mirroring each other. They shared a spirit of strength and holiness, which bound them together.[2] This type of bond transcends life itself.

A man was once traveling away from home on business in a far-off land. There, he was accused and found guilty of some crime against the king and was sentenced to death. The man asked the king to grant him some time to go back to his home and put his affairs in order, so that his family should not have to suffer even more. Afterward, he would return and accept his punishment. The king asked him, "How can I believe you will return at the appointed time and not just run away?"

The man replied that he has a friend who will come and take his

---

1. Shmuel I, chap. 19
2. Malbim, Shmuel I, 18:1

place and if he does not return, then that friend will stand in his stead. The idea that such a friendship existed piqued the king's curiosity. He agreed that if this sentenced man could find someone who would be willing to step in for him, in such a way, then he would let him go and settle his affairs.

The man sent a letter to his friend, explaining what had happened to him, and asking his friend to come and stand in for him. His friend arrived and happily agreed to take the place of his friend, freeing his friend to go to home and settle his affairs. The king was visibly impressed by the willingness of this friend to make such a sacrifice, but warned him that if his friend did not return in time, it would be he who would receive the death penalty. The man readily agreed and his friend set off for home.

Shortly before the agreed-upon date, the sentenced man, after spending time tying together his business, and giving his family parting words, left to return and receive his sentence. On the way back, he met delay after delay and became increasingly concerned that he might not make it back in time. Finally, he arrived on the appointed day, close to sunset, only to discover that his friend had already been taken toward the gallows. He ran to catch up, and found his friend, about to be hanged.

He yelled out for the proceedings to stop. It was he who was found deserving of death, not his friend. The king who was overseeing the punishment agreed and started to release his friend. The friend protested that the appointed time had arrived and his friend had not returned, so it was he who should be put to death, and his friend should be released. His friend in turn argued that it was he who had been found guilty of punishment and it was he who should receive it.

The king and his men had never seen such a level of devotion and loyalty between friends. The king was moved by their dedication to each other and called for a break to allow himself time to ponder what to do. An hour later, the king returned and presented his judgment: Both friends would be allowed to live, on condition that they make the king their friend as well.

Reflection

What is the quality of my friendships?

_____

_____

_____

_____

What would I be willing to sacrifice for the sake of my friendship?

_____

_____

_____

_____

What would others be willing to give for their friendship with me?

_____

_____

_____

_____

RELATIONSHIPS

There are three types of relationships in our lives: our relationship to others, our relationship to G-d, and our relationship to our selves. Being a complete person requires that we are whole with others, whole with our Creator, and whole with ourselves. Each of these is distinct and represents an essential component of our completeness.

Regarding which of these relationships is primary, there is a difference of opinion. Rebbe Yehuda taught: One who desires to be a pious person should become expert in the laws of damages.[1] Rava taught: One who desires to be a pious person should pursue the study of Ethics of our Fathers. And others say the study of blessings.[2]

Performing acts of kindness alone falls short of the level called piety. Rather, when we are careful to damage no one, directly, or indirectly, in any way, shape, or form, then we can be considered pious. This was the opinion of Rebbe Yehuda.

Rava said that the pathway to piety is by involvement in the teachings of Ethics of our Fathers. He understood that piety predominantly relates to our relationship with our selves. By learning and integrating the moral lessons of Ethics of our Fathers, we hone our character, developing an exquisite inner quality.

Others say that piety relates above all to one's relationship with the Creator. When G-d's name is frequently upon one's lips, blessing G-d for each and every item, then there is wholeness with the Creator. A

1. *Bava Kamma*, 30a
2. Ibid.

person who lives with such divine awareness, never separated from the name of G-d, is pious.[3]

Depending upon who we are, our path toward completion will be most effective through the doorway which is most natural to us. Those who are chiefly other-focused will choose the path of Rebbe Yehuda, developing skillful sensitivity in matters of damages. Those who are primarily self-focused will choose the way of Rava, refining their character traits through studying and applying the teachings of Ethics of our Fathers, laboring toward self-perfection. And those who are predominantly G-d-focused will pursue completion through concentrating on blessings.

Reflection

Which relationship do I relate to the most?

_____

_____

_____

_____

What are some examples of how this relationship is primary in my life?

_____

_____

_____

_____

What are some things I can do to develop greater wholeness in this area?

_____

_____

_____

_____

3. Maharal, *Chiddushei Aggados*, Bava Kama 30a

MALE AND FEMALE

"Male and female He created them."[1] The Midrash[2] teaches that initially, G-d created one being, who was both male and female. He then split them into two beings. Why did G-d not make man and woman two separate beings to begin with, if that is what He intended?

Animals were created as separate male and female creatures. This says something about the nature of their union. They couple to further the existence of their species, and then each picks up and goes on their way.

The connection between husband and wife is very different. It is not just about continuing the human race. It is about bonding with a piece of oneself; "bone from my bone, flesh of my flesh."[3] It is about a union that transcends the bounds of this world.

Creating us as one and then separating us into two set the stage for the type of relationship which man and woman are intended to have.[4] For this reason, husband and wife are referred to in Biblical Hebrew as "ish" and "isha." The similarity of their names is indicative of their oneness. In contrast, animals are referred to simply as "zachar" (male) and "nekeiva" (female), two dissimilar names.

We have a natural yearning to reach a more complete state and often seek this through relationships. This yearning and its expression comes from having once been in such a state of unity, and knowing, on some level, that this is where our wholeness is to be found. The joining of hus-

---

1. *Bereishis, 1:27; Bereishis, 5:2*
2. *Midrash Rabbah, 8:1*
3. *Bereishis, 2:23*
4. *Beis Elokim, Shaar HaYesodos, chap. 10*

band and wife is about two disconnected, disparate parts, reconnecting to form a greater whole.[5]

The more connected the parts become, the greater the wholeness. The more distance there is between the parts, the more work is needed to bring them together.[6] When we understand how much is dependent upon this unity, we can appreciate both why having it can be so pleasurable, and why being disconnected from it can be so painful.

This connection, or lack thereof, is not just about bonding with another. It is about returning a lost part of ourselves and becoming who we were meant to be. It is about becoming a whole person. Appreciating the weight of this relationship motivates us to invest in it appropriately.

Reflection

How do I perceive of the relationship between men and women?

_____

_____

_____

Where does this perception come from?

_____

_____

_____

How connected am I to my spouse (if you are married)?

_____

_____

_____

What are some things I can do to become more connected?

_____

_____

_____

5. Maharal, *Chiddushei Aggados*, Bava Basra,
6. Ramchal, *K'Lach Pischei Chochma*, Pesach 73

HOLDING BACK

When G-d created the world, He held back from making it perfect. He did this to make room for people, who are also imperfect. The reason for creating a world, and people in it, who are incomplete, is to give us the opportunity to be partners with G-d in bringing ourselves and the world to a more complete state through our efforts.[1] If we and the world were already perfect, our work would already be done, and there would be no reason for us or the world to exist.

G-d did this so that we could have ownership over our own completion. If we did not have to stretch ourselves and work to reach greater levels of refinement, the result would not be the same. The experience of receiving a handout (being made perfect) and the experience of earned achievement (working toward perfection) are worlds apart.[2]

There are many areas of life where we feel that because of greater age, experience, or knowledge, we are in a position to tell others how they should live their lives. Sometimes we may tell them what they should do. And, even if they are doing something we agree with, we may feel a need to tell them how they should be doing it. And perhaps, sometimes, we may even be right.

But, how often do we stunt the growth of another by over-functioning "for them"? How often do we limit others' learning and creative expression by not giving them more room to find their own way? If we would allow others to be imperfect more often, perhaps we would facilitate their growth, more than by trying to stop them from making mistakes.

1. Ramchal, *K'Lach Pischei Chochma*, 30
2. Ramchal, *Daas Tevunos*

When a parent is teaching a child to walk, they will likely take a step away from the child, to encourage the child to take a step forward. But wait, the child may fall, and the parent may not be able to catch the child. Yet, we all know that this is how a child learns to walk. And falling is part of that process.

By allowing the people in our lives to be imperfect once in a while, and giving them the space they need to be who they are, we may find that they get a lot further than if we try to "complete" them. Granted, there may be some falling along the way, but that is the way we learn to walk. A person who does not have the ability to walk on their own is sadly limited, despite the best of intentions.

Rabbi Yitzchak Blazer, the Rabbi of St. Petersburg, was one of the greatest students of Rabbi Yisrael Salanter. He was deliberating over a difficult communal issue and wrote his teacher a letter asking Rabbi Salanter to instruct him as to what he should do. His teacher wrote him back: "I could answer you, but doing so would make you smaller."

Rabbi Yisrael was a master at building people. He understood that in order for his student to rise to the levels he was capable of, he needed to make his own decisions, and take responsibility for them. This growth, Rabbi Yisrael deemed as being more important than whatever the "right" solution to the issue may have been. By giving his student space and not filling it with his own directives, Rabbi Yisrael was allowing his student to struggle with the issue on his own, deal with the uncertainty present, and proceed according to the best of his ability. The development which comes from dealing with this type of challenge would not have been possible if Rabbi Yisrael had answered his student's question.

Reflection

How often do I find myself giving others (especially those I care about) unsolicited advice or instruction?

_____

_____

_____

_____

How could I better be able to give others the space they need to grow?

_____

_____

_____

_____

What are the consequences of not giving others the space they need to develop themselves?

_____

_____

_____

_____

LACKING

Welcoming guests into one's home is greater than receiving the Divine presence. We learn this from Abraham, who interrupted his conversation with G-d to welcome guests into his home.[1]

Let us imagine for a moment that we are meeting with a powerful monarch. In the middle of our discussion, some passerby comes to the door. Would we say to a king of flesh and blood, "Hold on a minute, I am going to greet my guest, and then I will get back to you?"

Would this not be considered disrespectful toward a mortal king, much less the King of all kings?

The Maharal explains that it is a lacking in the glory of G-d for us to be in a state of lacking.[2] If Abraham did not address the needs of others, something fundamental would have been missing in him. In this light, Abraham's act was not one of disrespect, but rather an expression of honoring G-d, being true to what he needed to be whole.

In the laws of charity, there is a discussion of a person who was once wealthy and lost all their money. The law is that charity toward this person extends to even providing for servants to run before him. How can this qualify for charity? Are such things really necessary?

The answer is yes. For that person to feel whole, that is what he needs. And if so, this is also charity. The Torah is instructing us to lift him up to a place where he will not be lacking, subjective to who he is.

At the same time, the Talmud instructs[3] us that it is preferable to skin a dead carcass in the open marketplace, rather than need the charity

---

1. *Shabbos*, 127a
2. Maharal, *Chiddushei Aggados, Shabbos*, p. 68
3. *Pesachim*, 113a; *Bava Basra*, 110a

of others. As lowly as this professional option may seem, needing to depend upon others is even worse. There is lacking and there is lacking.

There are four main areas in life where we may find ourselves wanting:

(1) Financial
(2) Physical
(3) Emotional
(4) Spiritual

Some things are out of our control. A person may experience a tragedy and lose a limb. Aside from getting a prosthetic limb, there is very little that can be done to restore his loss. But how a person chooses to react to a situation is in their control, difficult as it may be.

Likewise, other life situations may have been due to numerous factors we had no power over. Whether we choose to leave things as they are or work to improve them is up to us. If our wealth, health, emotions, or spirituality are sub-par we can take action to improve their quality.

Our efforts may not always meet with success, but sometimes they will. It is unfathomable that G-d would bless us with a brain more powerful than the greatest supercomputer, and remarkable inner resources, if he did not intend for us to advance our lives. As the Maharal taught, G-d is glorified when His creations are not lacking.

Reflection

In which area(s) do I experience the greatest lacking?

_____

_____

How does this lacking affect me?

_____

_____

_____

What are some things I can do to address this lacking?

_____

_____

_____

AMBITION

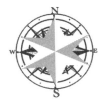

"And every person came whose heart lifted him up."[1]

Moses presented the Jewish people with the project of building the Tabernacle. It would require a tremendous degree of sophisticated artistry and craftsmanship to shape, build, and weave all the different parts of the Tabernacle. How could a nation of people who had spent their lives building pyramids be expected to accomplish such a task?

Nachmanides taught that despite the lack of anyone to learn such skilled work from, the people found within themselves a natural talent to do what was needed. Their hearts lifted them up with an inspiration to present themselves before Moses, saying, "I will do whatever you set forth."

If we look at the giants of the world, and almost all of the people who have achieved great wealth, practically all of them reached their accomplishments, in large part, due to a powerful ambition. Someone lacking in ambition cannot reach amazing heights. It is axiomatic that great people possess an amazing will to succeed.

The Torah describes the people who were successful in the holy work of building the Tabernacle. They came with uplifted hearts. They possessed natural ambition. Without any teachers or master craftsmen to show them the way, they came before Moses telling him that they would do whatever he instructed. This was the type of person who succeeded in their work and was able to build and complete the Tabernacle, the place where heaven and earth meet. When we consider the incredible amount of personal resources that we possess, it must be that we have them for some reason. If not for the accomplishment of some substan-

1. *Shemos*, 35:21

tial enterprise, why else would we have been given them? Yet, without a deep and powerful ambition, very little will come of our abilities.

Our Sages taught that a person is obligated to ask of themselves, "When will my actions reach those of Abraham, Isaac, and Jacob?"[2] When we seek to emulate gigantic mentors, this will bring us closer to reaching our own levels of top performance. Without this drive, our level of accomplishment and success falls sadly short of what we are capable of.[3]

As a case in point, a young boy was orphaned from his father at the age of seven. His mother worked two jobs to be able to hire for her son the best tutor in town to teach him Torah. One day, as the boy and his mother were walking home, they saw from the distance that their home was on fire. The mother began to weep. The son tried to comfort his mother and tell her that it was going to be Okay. G-d would take care of them. The mother responded to her son, "I am not crying about losing our home. I know that G-d will take care of us. I am crying about the book of our ancestry, which traces you back all the way to Yochanan HaSandlar. I wanted you to know the greatness you come from."

The boy looked at his mother and answered her with a confidence and maturity far beyond his years, "Don't worry, Mother, I will start a new book of ancestry. I will become the next Torah leader of the generation." True to his word, this little boy grew into the eminent Chassidic leader, the Maggid of Mezeritch.

Reflection

What are my ambitions?

_____

_____

_____

_____

2. *Tanna D'bei Eliyahu*, 25
3. Rabbi Yerucham Levovitz, *Daas Torah*, Vayakhel – Pekudei

How can I be more ambitious?

_____

_____

_____

_____

What are some things I can do to further my ambition(s)?

_____

_____

_____

_____

PERSEVERANCE

Rabbi Preida had a student who had a difficult time understanding. In order for this student to grasp something, Rabbi Preida needed to teach it to him four hundred times. One day, Rabbi Preida was asked to attend to some service. He taught this student four hundred times and the student still did not grasp the lesson. Rabbi Preida asked the student, "What was different about today, that you did not grasp it?" The student replied, "From the time that you were asked to attend to that service until now, I have been distracted by the thought that maybe you would stop the lesson and go." Rabbi Preida replied, "Focus, and I will teach you again." He repeated the lesson another four hundred times until the student understood.[1]

The first time that Rabbi Preida sat down with this student, what did he think after he had taught the lesson three hundred and ninety-nine times, and the student had still not grasped it? Did he not have something better to do with his time? Was he not a bit frustrated?

At the same time, we can ask about the student: What made him continue after having failed to understand so many times? Was it not a little embarrassing for him to sit with this great Sage and not grasp what was being taught, again and again? Why did he persist?

From the end of the story, we see two greatnesses: First, when the Rabbi heard that the student had not understood, even after having spent so much time and energy already, he did not get upset. He told the student to focus, and he started again, repeating the lesson another four hundred times. Second, when the student did not grasp, even after having been taught four hundred times, he was able to admit it and did not

1. *Eiruvin,* 54b

171

pretend to understand when he had not. What incredible persistence, both on the part of the Rabbi, and on the part of the student.

What enabled them to reach such levels of perseverance?

They were both committed to this student's gaining his share of the Torah. They both believed that if they tried long enough and hard enough, they would succeed. They had a goal and were determined to reach it. As a result, they were able to pay the price, again and again, to reach their aim.

When we fail to reach our goals, we need to be honest about how much commitment there was to reach them in the first place. How important did we consider our aim? How much determination did we bring to the task?

Oftentimes, we do not reach where we set out for because we are not willing to persevere. Whatever it was that we set our sights on, it was not valuable enough to pay the price of trying, again and again, for as long as it takes. Only when we feel that something is important enough will we find the necessary staying power to see it to the end.

Reflection

What are a few of my goals?

_____

_____

_____

_____

Which of them are valuable enough to me to pay the price of perseverance?

_____

_____

_____

_____

What is the price of my most valued goal?

_____

_____

_____

_____

SELF-DISCIPLINE

Who is mighty? He who conquers his inclination.[1] King Solomon taught that one who conquers his spirit is greater than one who conquers a city.[2] This is because a higher level of strength is required to be victorious over oneself, above and beyond that which is needed to be victorious over others.

King Solomon taught that there is a very real battle being waged between us and our appetites. Either we are in control or they are. There is no "in between."[3]

King Solomon is not advocating asceticism, instructing us to remove ourselves completely from all involvement in physicality. Rather, his message is that we need to channel our passions and desires in constructive ways, which serve us and others.[4] The bottom line is, who is sitting in the driver's seat: us or our appetites?

To rule over ourselves, we need to be in touch with all of our varied parts and know what each of them needs. This allows us to give each of our desires and needs their proper due, in the right way, at the right time, without shortchanging or overindulging any of them. When we do this, the totality of who we are is at our beck and call, when need be. Erring either in the direction of lacking or excess limits our effectiveness in getting the most out of ourselves.

This is similar to ruling a nation. When the leader understands what each of his subjects needs, and makes sure to give each their due, neither too much, nor too little, then in time of need, they will be ready

---

1. *Pirkei Avos*, chap. 4, Mishna 1
2. *Mishlei*, chap. 16
3. *Chovos HaLevavos*, Shaar Avodas HaElokim, chap. 4
4. *Tomer Devorah*, chap. 6

and willing to heed his call. If any of the subjects, however, are either neglected or spoiled, they will be less ready to do the leader's bidding.[5]

It is unrealistic to expect ourselves to be perfect at self-discipline from day one. Shaping our vision of who we would like to be and bringing it into actuality is a process. Similar to the process of sculpting a piece of clay into a magnificent sculpture, we start with an amorphous piece of material. Little by little we shape it, and it begins to take form. The work in progress goes through many stages and does not always look so good. But the sculptor knows that to bring forth the creation he aspires to, this is what is needed.

So too with ourselves, we need to appreciate that we are engaged in a creative process, which involves many stages of development. We need to gently, yet firmly, work our clay, shaping it step by step. And if we stay the course, eventually we will have a masterpiece – our own self mastery.

A great sculptor was once asked how he succeeded in making such beautiful works out of rock. He responded that the works were already there. He was just removing the stone that covered them.

Reflection

Which of my appetites are challenging to control?

_____

_____

What would help me to exert greater control?

_____

_____

How do I perceive my process of development?

_____

_____

What are some things I can do to develop myself better?

_____

_____

5. *Kuzari*, Maamar Shlishi, Os Beis - Heh

WORKING OUT OUR MIDDOS

Character traits are like muscles. The more we exercise them, the stronger they become.[1] This is true of both positive and negative traits.

To a large extent, our lives are ruled by the traits we have exercised the most.[2] They have become operating patterns that work almost automatically. A trigger is pulled and our pattern fires. And practice makes perfect.

But, perfect at what? is a question we need to ask. If the answer is, perfect at getting angry every time someone is inconsiderate of us, we might want to consider the cost of such perfection, and whether we want to keep investing in it. Every instance of following the same pattern, of responding in the same way, to the same things, is a deepening of our investment in being a certain way.

So, how can we choose to be different?

The first step is to take a step back and watch ourselves as we go about our day.[3] We will notice, if we pay attention, our automatic responses ready to go into action, as different occurrences happen throughout the course of the day. We can watch these knee-jerk responses without necessarily being swayed by them. This stepping back and observing enables us to gain an awareness of how we normally react to the events of our lives. It allows us to think about whether or not we like what we see, and avoid living a life of sliding along mindlessly.

The practice of stepping back and observing builds the strength necessary to disentangle ourselves from reactive patterns. It develops the

---

1. Ramban, *Devarim*, 29:18
2. Rabbeinu Yona, *Pirkei Avos*, 1:10, 1:18
3. *Mesilas Yesharim*, chap. 2

muscle of self-control by training our ability to observe our automatic responses without acting on them. Using a trait less often weakens its hold over us. As the Talmud teaches regarding avarice for physical pleasure, "There is a small organ that if it is satisfied will be starved, and if it is starved will be satisfied."[4]

The second step is to realize that just as exercising a negative trait, or not, affects its strength, so too with positive traits. If we want to grow in generosity, it is not enough to just think generous thoughts. We need to practice generosity.

It is better to give one coin one hundred times than it is to give one hundred coins one time. Even though the same amount of money is being given, at the end of the day, the effect on the giver is not the same. The person who performs a hundred acts of giving will have become a more generous person than the one who only performed one act of giving, generous as his donation may have been. To a large extent, we are made by our actions.[5]

The students of Rav Adda Bar Ahava asked him how he merited living such a long life. He answered, "In my lifetime, I never got upset in my home. I never walked in front of someone who was greater than me. I did not meditate on the Torah in filthy places. I did not walk four cubit feet without thinking about Torah and wearing Tefillin.[6] I did not sleep in the house of study. And, I did not rejoice in the misstep of my peers, or call any of them by a nickname.[7]

Reflection

What are some of my habits?

_____

_____

_____

_____

4. *Sukkah*, 52b
5. *Sefer HaChinuch*, Mitzvah 99
6. phylacteries
7. *Taanis*, 20b

Are they working for me?

_____

_____

_____

_____

Which habits would I like to develop?

_____

_____

_____

_____

What can I do to develop them?

_____

_____

_____

_____

QUIETING

Developing ourselves requires a measure of strategy. Rabbi Kalonymos Kalman Shapira, the Rebbe of the Warsaw Ghetto, taught a very powerful method for developing our character.[1] He gave a close student the following practical instructions:

"Look at your thoughts for several minutes, simply observing what you are thinking.

You will slowly begin to feel your mind emptying from these thoughts, and you will notice that they have slowed from their regular flow.

"Then begin to recite one verse, such as, 'The Lord, our G-d, is truth,' in order to attach your mind, which is empty of other thoughts, to one thought of holiness.

"Afterward, it is possible to ask for your needs, regarding a trait which is in need of refinement, whether it be in strengthening your awareness of G-d, or in experiencing greater love and awe of the Creator."

The student wrote: At that time, I merited to hear an example of this from the Admur (our master and teacher) regarding strengthening one's awareness of G-d. The Admur began:

"I believe with complete faith that the Creator is the only existence in the world. There is no existence outside of His Existence. And the entire world and everything in it is only a refraction of the Light of G-d."

He repeated this several times. But he stressed that when doing this, one should not speak forcefully, because the purpose is to quiet one's thoughts, and by saying something forcefully, a person's "selfness" will be awakened. On the contrary, do this in a very gentle way.

---

1. *Derech HaMelech*, p. 451

I also merited hearing the Admur speak concerning love of G-d. This is what he said:

"I greatly want to be close to G-d, blessed be He. I greatly want to feel closeness to the Awesome Creator."

The Admur taught that this method can be used to improve all of a person's character flaws. Not with a focus on the negative, but rather with a focus on the positive behavior which is the opposite of the negative attribute. For example, a person suffering from laziness should not speak about distancing themselves from laziness, but rather about acquiring alacrity and industriousness.

The Admur explained in the following way:

If you see a small child crying and you tell him not to cry, the more you tell him not to cry, the more he cries. You get whatever you focus on. If you focus on the negative, that is what you get; so instead, focus on the positive trait you want to develop.

Reflection

What strategies have I tried for developing my character?

_____

_____

_____

What has been more effective and what has been less effective?

_____

_____

_____

Which trait(s) would I like to strengthen?

_____

_____

_____

What can I do to develop it/them?

_____

_____

_____

SUFFERING

In the days of prophecy, G-d would communicate to us through the prophets. They would relay His message and let us know where we needed to do some fixing. Even with the cessation of prophecy, we were not left without direction, though. We were left with another type of prophecy – suffering.[1]

For better or for worse, there are few things which are as instructive as suffering. We tend to look at suffering a bit simplistically: "I must have messed up and now G-d is punishing me." But this perspective misses the point.

Suffering is like a prophet. It points out with specificity where we have taken a wrong turn, and in what area we need to do some work. The suffering we endure is directly related to where we have erred.

There is no such thing as arbitrary suffering. There is a direct correlation between what G-d sends us and what we need to address in our lives. Samson is a particularly vivid example of this. He strayed after his eyes, and the Philistines gouged out his eyes. Absalom is another good example. He put on airs because of his beautiful hair, and his hair got caught in the branches of a tree, leaving him hanging, as he was trying to flee for his life.[2] By examining the nature of the suffering which G-d sends to us, we can discover what we need to pay more attention to.

Rabbi Yoel Teitelbaum, the Satmar Rebbe, lived with this understanding. As he was walking home with his assistant, they started to ascend the stone steps to the Rebbe's home. The Rebbe slipped and fell. The attendant asked the Rebbe if he was Okay. The Rebbe responded that he

---

1. *Toras Avraham*, p. 28
2. *Sotah*, 9b

was. The attendant waited for the Rebbe to get up, but the Rebbe made no move to do so. The attendant asked once again if the Rebbe was perhaps hurt. The Rebbe answered that he was not and continued to sit where he had fallen. The assistant, after waiting a few more moments, asked the Rebbe, "If you are not hurt, why are you not getting up?"

The Rebbe answered, "What will it help to get up if I do not yet know why I have fallen?"

The Rebbe was sitting and contemplating why he had fallen. It was clear to him that there was a reason why he had ended up on the ground. And it made no sense for him to get up until he understood what that reason was. Getting up without doing so would be missing the point.

Reflection

What are some examples of suffering I have experienced?

_____

_____

_____

What can I learn from these experiences?

_____

_____

_____

Is there something I need to address in my life right now?

_____

_____

_____

If so, what are some things I can do about it?

_____

_____

_____

LEPROSY

The segment discussing the metzora (leper) is one of the most encouraging in the Torah. Tzaraas (a spiritual form of leprosy) is a physical manifestation of a spiritual ailment. Because someone used their power of speech in a destructive way, turning it against their fellow man, their physicality is afflicted, reflecting their spiritual state. Our Sages teach that speaking derogatorily of others is worse than the three cardinal sins a Jew is required to sacrifice his life for rather than transgress: Idolatry, Illicit relations, and murder. Furthermore, a leper is considered as a dead person.[1]

And at the same time, this is not the end of the story. Despite the metzora's having seriously messed up, as human beings sometimes do, the Torah has a prescription for purity. The metzora comes to the priest and is instructed to take some time out – to separate himself, to be alone with himself, and reflect on who he is and who he wants to be. What is the nature of his relationships and how would he like them to be. The tzaraas (leprosy) heals and the priest gives the metzora a path of action with which to achieve purification.

The metzora brings two birds, which symbolize incessant chirping, and which call the metzora to reflect on how he had become careless in his speech. He brings cedar wood, from the highest of trees to remind him that he is not so "high" that he can afford to speak ill of others. He brings a crimson thread and hyssop, which symbolize that the path of healing is through humbling oneself, and lowering his place like that of the worm, used for the red dye, and the hyssop.[2]

---

1. *Nedarim*, 64b
2. Rashi, Metzora

The next stage of purification requires him to shave the hair anywhere it is found on the outside of the body. Hair is found where there is the greatest life force. The hair on one's head, for example, is next to the brain – which, although it weighs only a few pounds, uses up about twenty-five percent of our oxygen supply. Likewise, men have an abundance of hair around the mouth, the organ of speech. Speech is the crowning faculty of man, as Onkelos translates in Genesis, that when G-d blew into man a spirit of life, it meant that He made him a speaking being. There is hair under the arms, near our vital organs. And there is hair near our reproductive organs.

It seems that this metzora used his life force in a maladaptive way. As a result, he became sick. Perhaps, now that he is starting anew, he needs to give himself a fresh, clean start, to the extent that even his physical growth should be in accordance with his new identity.

The path to purification continues, elevating the metzora to the point where he can rejoin his people in wholeness. The metzora teaches us that it is possible to lift ourselves up from even a place akin to death. It is possible to reconnect to our higher selves if we lost that somewhere along the way. G-d is teaching us here that He is not looking to cut us off, or to punish us. He is looking to bring us close to Him, and provide us a path back when we have lost the way.

Reflection

How careful am I in my speech?

_____

_____

_____

Where have my sensitivities become dulled?

_____

_____

_____

What would help me to regain sensitivity?

_____

_____

_____

FORGIVENESS

The Shulchan Aruch (Code of Jewish Law) rules[1] that when someone comes to ask of us forgiveness, we should not be cruel and refuse. On one level, this is simply a piece of good advice. Providence has a rule called "measure for measure."[2] As you do unto others, so too will be done unto you. When we are forgiving of others, G-d is forgiving of us.

But there is another facet worth considering. When we hold on to our grievances against others, we are in fact punishing ourselves. We are actively cultivating a swamp of toxicity within ourselves. And each time we rehash, and churn over the events of how we were wronged, we dive headfirst into that swamp. As one thinker ironically expressed, "It is like taking poison and expecting the other person to die."

In the order of the recitation of Shema ("Hear O Israel") before bedtime, there is a declaration of forgiveness in which we let go of all our grievances, forgiving all of those who may have wronged us. Our Sages were acutely aware of the price of holding on to grudges, including its power to rob us of a good night's sleep. Forgiving others at the end of each day helps us to return our soul each night in peace.

Rabbi Yisrael Salanter, who dedicated his life to refining and understanding human character, understood better than most how destructive bearing grudges can be. He was once traveling on a train with a young man. The young man, not recognizing his traveling partner, was incredibly rude, to the point of being insulting. When they reached their destination, the young man saw the huge welcoming party which had

---

1. *Orach Chaim*, 606:1
2. *Sotah*, 9a, Rashi D"H *L'k'middah*

gathered to greet his traveling companion. He was horrified when he realized whom he had insulted.

He found out where Rabbi Salanter was staying and went to ask his forgiveness. Rabbi Salanter received him warmly and asked him about the nature of his trip. The young man replied that he came to be tested as a shochet (ritual slaughterer). Rabbi Salanter sent him to a relative of his, who was a prominent Rabbi in the town, to be examined. The young man's proficiency was found to be quite lacking. Rabbi Salanter hired a very learned and expert ritual shochet to teach the young man, at his own great expense, until the young man was able to receive the certification he desired.

Rabbi Salanter was asked why he went to such lengths to help this young man, whom he hardly even knew. He replied that when he was traveling with him, he had been insulted. Although he had forgiven the young man immediately, he was concerned that perhaps his forgiveness had been incomplete, and that he had held on to a vestige of resentment. In order to counteract this, he went out of his way to act in kindness to the young man, to eradicate any ill will he may have felt toward him.

Sometimes the hardest person to forgive is oneself. To forgive ourselves for mistakes we may have made. To forgive ourselves for opportunities missed. To forgive ourselves for not being wiser or better in some way, shape, or form. As harmful as bearing a grudge against others can be, doing the same to ourselves is no less damaging.

It stands to reason that if forgiving others is so valuable, forgiving ourselves should not be any less so. As the commandment to "love our neighbor as we love ourselves"[3] suggests: in order to really love others and be kind to them, we must first be able to love and show kindness toward ourselves. This includes being able to forgive ourselves.

Reflection

Who do I have a hard time forgiving?

_____

_____

_____

_____

---

3. *Vayikra*, 19:18

How does this affect me?

_____

_____

_____

_____

What would help me to be more forgiving?

_____

_____

_____

_____

COUNTING

One of the most destructive forces known to man is the thought: I do not count. The Jewish people are about to journey into the desert. They are about to wage a difficult spiritual war with the forces of darkness (referred to symbolically as the snake, the seraph, and the scorpion[1]). How does G-d prepare them? He counts them.

We only count things which matter to us. In the laws of Kashrus, when dealing with mixtures of the prohibited and the permitted, something which is counted individually is not considered negligible even if mixed with many other things. The reason is that because of its importance, we cannot consider it null, even if it is a tiny minority.

By counting us, G-d is expressing, "Each and every one of you matters. Each and every one of you is valuable and important. Each and every one of you has a special mission to fulfill that is yours alone. You count. You are the farthest thing possible from negligible."

The most critical factor in winning a war is strengthening one's heart.[2] The priest instructs the nation before going into battle: "Do not let your hearts become weak."[3] Similarly, King Solomon instructs us concerning our spiritual struggles: "Do not back down in the face of anything,"[4] And the Talmud explains: "The beginning of defeat is running away."[5]

When a person sees himself as valuable and capable of accomplishing greatness, he is then able to overcome even the most challenging opponents. Therefore, G-d commands the Jewish people to be counted.

1. *Tikkunei Zohar*, 125a
2. *Shem MiShmuel*, Bamidbar
3. *Devarim*, 20
4. *Mishlei*, 30:30
5. *Sotah*, 44b

And so too, each time we find the Jews about to go to war, either physical or spiritual, we find that G-d calls for a counting (i.e., before they enter the land of Israel to fight the seven nations). Someone who is counted is important. Somebody who feels he matters fights a different kind of fight than someone who feels he is insignificant.

There is a Torah law concerning a person who is killed by the side of the road. We measure which city is the closest one to where the body was found. The elders of that city break the neck of a calf and wash their hands over the body and say, "Our hands have not shed the blood of this person."

Was there really a suspicion that these venerable Sages spent their free time murdering travelers? Rashi explains that they did not see this person and let him leave their city without providing him some food and an escort as he left the city. We see from here that there is a connection between not providing such support and killing a person.

What does this mean?

When a person is given food and an escort upon leaving a city, a message is being given: You are somebody worth giving food to. You are someone worth escorting. You have value. A person who feels they are worth something will put up a different kind of fight, when attacked, than someone who feels they are worth nothing. If the elders of the city had ignored this basic human need to be considered, on some level, they would have been responsible for killing this person.

How we choose to treat others can be life-giving or life-taking. The words we use and the care we show go much farther than we realize. By taking responsibility for how we treat others and committing ourselves to letting others know how much they matter, we can emulate G-d's attribute of making others count.

The Chazon Ish, one of the great Sages of the past generation, lived in Bnei Brak. One day he saw through his window the Brisker Rav, another great Torah figure, passing in front of his home. He got up quickly, put on his best attire, and prepared himself to give this remarkable man the proper greeting.

As the man got closer, he realized that it was not the Brisker Rav. Nonetheless, he went out and greeted this fellow Jew with the same respect and enthusiasm as if he was the Brisker Rav. Those in his home were a bit confused as to what they were witnessing. Why was the Chazon Ish exerting such efforts for this person?

The Chazon Ish later explained to them, "I had prepared myself to greet the Brisker Rav with the respect which is due. In truth, it is proper to greet every Jew with such honor. Now, that I had finally prepared myself to do so, should I waste the opportunity to great another Jew the way I should."

Reflection

What are some things which make me feel like I count?

_____

_____

_____

_____

What are some things I do which make other people feel like they count?

_____

_____

_____

_____

How often do I do these types of things?

_____

_____

_____

_____

What else can I do to make people feel like they count?

_____

_____

_____

_____

A BEAUTIFUL PATH

Deborah the prophetess tells Barak to gather an army of ten thousand men and go to war with Sisra, the enemy general who was oppressing the Jews. He replies that he will only go if she comes with him. She answers that she will go with him, "but your beauty will not be on the path you are walking. Rather, Sisra will be delivered into the hands of a woman." And that is what happened. The victory in battle was attributed to Deborah going to war, and Sisra was killed by Yael, another woman.[1]

What is going on here? Why did Barak refuse to go without Deborah? And what does her reply mean – "your beauty will not be found on such a path"?

Barak had two concerns[2]:

One concern was that he would not be able to assemble an army on his own. He was afraid that the men would not listen to him and that only if Deborah came would they join him.

The second was that he was afraid his merits were insufficient for him to be victorious in battle. Only if she came and added her merit, then there would be victory.

Barak's concerns sound pretty legitimate. What was the meaning of Deborah's response, which indicates that something was wrong with his request?

Rav Tzaddok HaKohen taught that just as a person has an obligation to believe in G-d, so too they have an obligation to believe in themselves. A person needs to believe that his soul comes from the Source of all life,

1. *Shoftim*, chap. 4
2. *Malbim*

and that G-d takes pleasure in a person when they perform His will.[3] If Barak had believed in himself a little more, he would have been able to follow through on the prophetess's directive independently. In doing so, he would have been responsible for revealing G-d's glory and realizing his own potential. Because he did not, his beauty remained buried, even to himself.

Rabbi Naphtali of Amsterdam once said to his teacher and mentor, Rabbi Yisrael Salanter, "If I had the mind of the Shaagas Aryeh (a tremendous Torah genius), the heart of the Yesod VaShoresh HaAvoda (the author of a great work on serving G-d with deep levels of attachment) and the character of Rebbe (Rabbi Yisrael Salanter, a paragon of character development), then I could serve G-d."

The great Rabbi Yisrael Salanter replied, "With your mind, with your heart, and with your character, you can serve G-d." This was not an empty platitude. It was a profound piece of wisdom: When a person comprehends the tremendous treasure they possess inside, they are empowered to walk a beautiful path in which they reveal their own light.

Reflection

How much do I believe in myself?

_____

_____

What has influenced how much I believe in myself?

_____

_____

_____

What would help me to believe in myself a little bit more?

_____

_____

What would I accomplish if I really believed in myself?

_____

_____

3. *Tzidkas HaTzaddik*, 194

DIGGING FOR TREASURE

Every Jewish soul was present when G-d gave the Torah on Mt. Sinai.[1] To each of these souls was given a special portion of the Torah which is theirs alone. Realizing who we are has everything to do with finding this portion.

"If a person says, 'I toiled and I found,' believe him."[2] When we exert ourselves to learn Torah we will discover that we are naturally drawn to certain areas above others.[3] By listening to this intuition and following it we can regain what was once ours. Although effort is involved, it is an effort to find something which is already part of us. For this reason, when we learn something that really resonates with us, there is a sense of having always known it, even though we may have just heard it for the first time.

There is a vast difference between a person who has lost a fortune, and a person who possesses a fortune, but it is buried deep in the ground.[4] The former may be depressed and lose hope. He has no idea how to recoup his loss. The latter is concerned. He knows that he has a lot of work ahead of him if he wants to reach his treasure. But, the more concerned he becomes, the harder he works, taking strength and joy that he is on the way to claiming his fortune.

Discovering our portion in Torah is like digging for treasure buried deep in the ground. The ground is us. And the digging is about working through layer upon layer of challenge to find our share of the Torah. We

1. *Shem Olam* (Kisvei Chafetz Chaim, 1:13) quoting the GRA
2. *Megillah*, 6b
3. *Avodah Zarah*, 19a
4. *Chovas HaTalmidim*, chap. 2

are diggers who know where our treasure is. And if we keep on digging, we will reveal it.

Reflection

Which area(s) of Torah study draws me the most?

_____

_____

_____

_____

What are some things I can do to excel in this portion of the Torah?

_____

_____

_____

_____

What are some of the challenges I face in learning Torah?

_____

_____

_____

_____

What are some things I can do to overcome these challenges?

_____

_____

_____

_____

OUTER WORK

In addition to our inner work, our outer work also needs to match who we are. The Chovos HaLevavos teaches that each person is drawn to a specific vocation. He explains that G-d planted within every person a love and affection for a certain type of work or trade. Man is similar in this respect to other living beings in whom G-d planted instinctual drives. For example, a cat was given a nature to capture mice. A hawk was given a nature to capture birds. Certain fowl only capture fish. So too, G-d planted within each and every type of living thing a nature and a desire, which serves as a means to acquire their livelihood.

Furthermore, G-d matched the physiology and the character of the different living beings to their livelihood as well. A bird that captures fish is born with a long beak and extended thighs. A lion, which tears apart other animals for food, is made with powerful teeth and claws. The makeup of animals who feed on plants is quite different.

Similar to the animal kingdom, each person is suited to a particular business, trade, or craft, according to their physical and emotional makeup. Therefore, one who feels a particular attraction to a specific type of work, and his body is suited for it, should take notice. If he is able to go through the necessary effort required to pursue that field, he should make it a means with which to acquire a livelihood. He should engage in it with desire – and trust in G-d to ensure his livelihood all the days of his life.[1]

How often do people choose career paths because of considerations, other than what attracts them, and what matches their natural resources?

It makes sense on a natural level as well, that in the endeavors we

---

1. *Chovos Halevavos*, Shaar Habitachon, chap. 3

are attracted to, and suited to, our levels of performance will be much greater. So why do we look elsewhere?

Oftentimes, profession is used as a means to gain approval or status. Sometimes, our motives are financial. Either way, when we choose to dedicate the hours of our day, and the years of our life, to a livelihood, is being true to who we are any less important than these other concerns? If we lose ourselves, what have we gained?

Rabbi Levi Yitzchak of Berditchev once saw a man rushing through the marketplace in great haste. He asked the man, "What are you running after?"

The man answered, "I am running after my sustenance and livelihood."

Rabbi Levi Yitzchak replied, "And how do you know that your livelihood is before you, that you are running after it to catch it? Maybe it is behind you, and you are running away from it?"

We can invest large portions of our lives and ourselves in paths that we never cared that much for. And possibly worse, never develop our innate potential in areas that would have been much more personally, and possibly financially, rewarding. We owe it to ourselves to listen carefully to our own voice, and at least hear its message.

Reflection

Is there some type of work that I am particularly attracted to and that suits me?

_____

_____

_____

What would it take to pursue this path?

_____

_____

_____

Am I willing to make this investment?

_____

_____

TRUST

There was a young lady who was traveling to her parents' home. On the way, she fell into a pit. Along came a young man who made her the following proposition: If I lift you out of the pit, will you marry me? She agreed. Afterward, they swore to one another that he would not marry anyone else, and she would not marry anyone else. They said, "Who will be our witnesses?" Just then, a weasel was passing by the pit. They said, "These two, the pit and the weasel, shall be our witnesses." Then, each went on their way.

The young lady remained true to her oath, but the young man did not. He married another woman and had a son with her. One day, a weasel came along, bit the son, and he died. Soon after, another son was born to this couple. This son fell into a pit and died. This man's wife could not help but notice that something very strange was going on. She had had two sons who had died such uncommon deaths. She asked her husband, "What is happening here?" He told her the whole story of helping the young lady out of the pit, their oath to one another, and their "witnesses." She said to her husband, "If so, go back and marry that girl." He wrote his wife a divorce, and went to marry the girl he had lifted from the pit.[1]

The Talmud remarks: "See how great those of faith are. Those who placed their trust in a pit and a weasel had such effect, all the more so, those who place their trust in G-d."[2]

In the physical world, we understand the law of gravity. What goes up must come down. When we throw a ball up into the air, we have no

1. *Tosfos*, Taanis, D"H *B'Chulda*, 8a
2. *Taanis*, 8a

expectation that it will stay there. There is a specific cause-and-effect relationship, which we are aware of and can use to our benefit.

Similar to the physical world, the spiritual world also has laws. Once put in place, they operate as designed. One of these laws is the law of trust. That which we place our trust in effects consequences. The couple placed their trust in a weasel and a pit, and there were very real outcomes which this affected.

This goes even further. The Vilna Gaon is quoted as saying, "If a thief, in the middle of his break-in, would be able to completely fill himself with trust in G-d, he will succeed in his thievery."[3] When a person reaches that place called trust, and attaches himself to it, he can use it to carry out his desire. Trust was invested with a power to bring success, regardless of the person's idea of success. Nature is nature, and once established will run its course.

Some people trust that they will not succeed. Time and again, they prove themselves right. Others believe that, with G-d's help, they will succeed. Although it may take a number of tries, they are usually right as well. It would be wise to think about what we put our trust in. In doing so, we can invest our power of trust more beneficially.

Reflection

Where do I place my trust?

_____

_____

_____

_____

What can I do to increase my level of trust in G-d?

_____

_____

_____

_____

3. *Shiurei Daas*, vol. 1, p. 59

Do I trust that I will succeed?

_____

_____

_____

_____

How does this belief impact me?

_____

_____

_____

_____

MONEY

"Why does he go up a steep ramp and hang from a tree, risking his life? – For money."[1]

A person is willing to put himself in the most precarious of situations when it comes to money. Why is it that when it comes to this item, a person is willing to risk so much?

The desire for money is distinct from all other desires. When it comes to desiring honor, or some physical pleasure, the person is dealing with a specific want. When it comes to money, a person is dealing with the totality of all their wants.

Through acquiring wealth, a person imagines that he will be able to satisfy all his desires. Whatever pleasures he feels he is missing, he will be able to have. Honor, peace, and tranquility will all be his. Since so much depends upon money, his self-sacrifice for it is likewise so great.[2]

With this, we can understand better why money in Biblical Hebrew is called "kessef." Kessef comes from the word "kissufin," which means a deep yearning and desiring for something. At its root, money is connected with the quality of desiring, itself.[3]

We see how deep this desiring goes in the laws of bodily damages. If a person puts out his friend's eye, the Torah instructs us that he shall pay, "An eye for an eye."[4] Our Sages explain this to mean that he has to pay for the value of the eye.[5] On the surface, there seems to be little equivalence between that which has been taken and that which is being paid.

---

1. *Bava Metzia*, 112a
2. *Toras Avraham*, p. 20
3. *Likkutei Halachos*, Choshen Mishpat, Hilchos Arev, Halacha 3
4. *Shemos*, 21:24
5. *Bava Kama*, 84a

The Torah also refers to money as "damim" – blood. This is indicative of the connection that exists between one's very being, their blood, and money. When we consider the amount of suffering a person is willing to endure for money, paying for the loss of a limb with money becomes more comprehensible. Since one is willing to give of their blood for money, money is similarly the payment imposed for causing a loss of blood.[6]

Appreciating the weight that money has helps us to stand outside it and view how it impacts us. By being aware of how our relationship with wealth affects us, and perhaps why, we can evaluate if our responses to it are serving us or not. We can then choose what we are willing to pay for money, and what is simply not worth the cost.

Reflection

What am I prepared to give to acquire money?

_____

_____

_____

_____

What am I not prepared to give?

_____

_____

_____

_____

6. *Yismach Moshe*, Mishpatim

MASTER OR SERVANT

Being who one is – and becoming – all that one can be, demands a level of self-respect. As simple as this seems, even the greatest people can falter in this area. When Jacob leaves the house of Lavan, he sends his brother, Esau, a message. In it, he refers to himself as "your servant Jacob."[1] Our Sages take great issue with Jacob over this. How could this righteous person lower himself before the wicked Esau?

"Like a muddied spring and a ruined fountain, so is a righteous one who bows before an evildoer."[2] The Midrash teaches that G-d said to Jacob, "He [Esau] was going on his way, and you send him a message saying 'So says your servant Jacob'!?"[3]

At the time that Jacob called Esau "My master," G-d said to him, "You lowered yourself and called Esau, eight times, 'my master' – by your life, I will raise eight kings from his children before yours . . ."[4] His children will be rulers while yours are servants.

What was the issue exactly?

The world was created to reflect the glory of G-d.[5] When the righteous humble themselves before evildoers, it seems to indicate that there is a reason for existence outside of fulfilling the will of G-d. For Jacob to give such an impression, even with the best of reasons, signifies a tragic loss of perspective.

Rabbi Yeruchem Levovitz explains that Jacob is punished measure

---

1. *Bereishis*, 32:5
2. *Mishlei* 25:26
3. *Midrash Rabbah*, 85:2
4. Midrash, ibid.
5. *Isaiah*, 43:7; *Rabbeinu Yona* on Mishlei 16:4

for measure.[6] You made him (Esau) a master over yourself – as a result, you are his servant. Whoever flatters an evildoer will eventually fall into their hands.[7]

In contrast, we find in the case of Abraham that in all his transactions with the people of Cheis, over the purchase of a burial tomb for his wife Sarah, even though he needed them and behaved respectfully toward them, he never calls them "my master." On the contrary, they say to him: "Listen, our master, you are a prince of G-d among us."[8]

It is interesting to note that those who flatter the most are often those who are respected the least. There is a natural tendency to want to find favor in the eyes of others. But it is important to ask ourselves at what price, and what are we gaining for the price we are paying.

Reflection

Whom do I seek to find favor with?

_____

_____

_____

What is the price I am paying?

_____

_____

_____

What am I gaining for what I am paying?

_____

_____

_____

What would be a better way of accomplishing my objective?

_____

_____

_____

6. *Daas Torah*
7. *Sotah*, 41b
8. *Daas Torah*, VaYishlach

AFTER THE FALL

Rebbe Shlomo Karliner taught that as much as the evil inclination is interested in making a person fall, it is even more interested in the depressed feelings which follow the fall. It is easy to misinterpret this teaching as saying, "Don't get down after you fall, because that is what the evil inclination wants. Fight it by not feeling bad after you make a mistake." This is a gross oversimplification of a profound insight.

Rebbe Shlomo was teaching that after a person falls, it is very easy to get depressed. What is this depression about?

When we fall, it is very natural to identify ourselves as people who fail. It is easy to see ourselves in a negative light and have a poor estimation of our value and our ability to ever do better. If we believe this about ourselves, then we have little chance of lifting ourselves up, much less developing our unique potential. This is the endgame of the evil inclination, totally disempowering us. Its explicit mission is to block us from bringing the light into the world that we are here to reveal.

Rebbe Nachman of Breslov taught that if we let go of ourselves and give in to this negative self-impression, the evil inclination has won. Instead, we need to hold on tight and pull ourselves up. We must remember that as long as the candle (of the soul) is lit, there is still time to fix. If we believe we can ruin ourselves, believe that we can rectify ourselves.[1]

Being a success in life is not about never making a mistake. In fact, it is inevitable not to fall sometimes, as the verse teaches, "There is no righteous person who does only good and never sins."[2] Instead, the

---

1. *Likutei Moharan*, Mahadura Basra, Siman 112
2. *Koheles*, 7:20

formula for greatness is, "Seven times, a righteous person falls and gets up."[3]

A well-lived life is a process. It is about getting up, time and again, learning from our mistakes, and moving on. The biggest mistake we can ever make is instead of picking ourselves up and moving forward, we allow ourselves to get stuck in the mistake.

Reflection

What are some examples of times I have fallen?

_____

_____

_____

_____

What happens to me when I fall?

_____

_____

_____

_____

What are some things I can do to recover more effectively?

_____

_____

_____

_____

3. *Mishlei*, 24:16

GETTING UP

A famous story is told of a potential convert who came before Shammai, considering conversion. He said to Shammai, "I will convert to Judaism on condition that you teach me the whole Torah while I am standing on one foot." Shammai replied by chasing him away with a builder's rod. This potential convert then went to Hillel, and repeated his desire to become Jewish, if Hillel could teach him the whole Torah while he stood on one foot. Hillel replied, "That which is hateful unto you, do not do unto others. This is the whole Torah. The rest is commentary, go and learn."[1]

What was a Sage like Shammai doing, chasing away this person with a builder's rod? Could he not have found a more subtle way to communicate his message?

The potential convert was telling Shammai that he wanted to be Jewish. But only on condition that he would have only ups and not downs. ("Only on one foot" = only with a foot up.) He only wanted to have good days.[2]

Shammai chased him away with a builder's rod. He was communicating that the world has built into it ups and downs, night and day, good and bad. (The builder's rod = the way the world is built.) The Torah, which is the blueprint of creation, cannot be observed on only one foot, only from a place of ups and no downs.

Rebbe Nachman of Breslov was asked how he reached his lofty levels. He replied that even if he fell a hundred times in a single day, he got up and started anew each time. As long as we practice a little self-

1. *Shabbos*, 31a
2. *Mekor Mayim Chaim*, Bereishis

acceptance, understand that falling is part of life, and refuse to give up, the possibility of lifting ourselves up is open, no matter how many times we may fall.

Reflection

What are some examples of bad days I have had?

_____

_____

_____

_____

What messages do I read into what is happening?

_____

_____

_____

_____

How else can I look at what is happening?

_____

_____

_____

_____

SELF-TALK

If we listen carefully, we may notice the ongoing dialogue we carry on with ourselves. As we go about our lives, there is an inner commentator that gives its take on how well it thinks we are doing. Sometimes the commentary can be pretty harsh and leave us feeling put down. If others would speak to us this way, we would probably not want to spend much time with them. And yet, we live with this voice, day in and day out, and rarely, if ever, question its authority.

Where this voice comes from is far less important than our identifying with it.[1] As long as we accept its message as an accurate portrayal of who we are, it will continue to bring us down. Feelings of failure and worthlessness can often do more harm than any mistakes we may have made.

By focusing on the good points we possess, it is possible to change how we relate to ourselves and to the world.[2] It is impossible that we have not done some good in our lives. And even if we can find some fault with that too, there were still be some rays of light that were present.

When we collect one bright point after another, seeing the merit that we possess, our hearts become lifted with joy. Joy strengthens us. It gives us the encouragement we need to better ourselves and move in a more positive direction.

These points of merit join together like solitary notes in a beautiful piece of music. Their song lifts our heart and carries it to a higher place, above and beyond any negativity. It is a melody of holiness connecting us to where we are from, enveloping us in its delight.

---

1. *Chovos HaLevavos*, Shaar Yichud HaMaaseh, chap. 2
2. *Likutei Moharan*, 1:282

We get more of whatever we focus on. If we focus on how inadequate we are, we will get more of that. If we focus on the light we have revealed, we will also get more of that.

The first focus leaves us feeling down and helpless. The second focus encourages and empowers us. Considering the difference between these two possibilities it serves us better to communicate with ourselves in a way that lifts us up.

Reflection

Take a few minutes and notice this inner dialogue. What is it saying?

_____

_____

_____

_____

How helpful is it?

_____

_____

_____

_____

How accurate is it?

_____

_____

_____

_____

What can I do to lift up the content of this dialogue?

_____

_____

_____

_____

COMPASSION

In Psalms we read that G-d "heals the broken-hearted and salves their wounds."[1] In the blessing before the recitation of Shemah in the morning prayers, G-d is referred to as, "our Father, the Father of compassion." It is interesting to note that despite the commandment to "walk in His ways"[2] – to emulate His attributes[3] – when it comes to how we relate to our own lives, there is often a significant lack of compassion.

It is common when faced with difficult circumstances to feel as if that is the whole picture. This is how life is and that is it. When the clouds are overhead, the sun will never shine.

When this happens, it is important to remember the story of a king who asked a wise man to bring him something which, when he feels sad, will cheer and comfort him, and when things are going well, will help him to remain sober. The wise man brought the king a ring which had written upon it three words: Gam Zeh Yaavor (This too shall pass). In troubled times, the king could look at the ring and remember that this difficulty would pass and be cheered and comforted, and when things were going well, he would look at the ring and not get carried away, remembering that "this too shall pass."[4]

Reminding ourselves that whatever difficulty we may be experiencing will pass is an act of self-compassion. It is a gift of perspective that we give ourselves, which enables us to better cope with trying circumstances. Beating ourselves up for not being different and for not having done things differently is generally not very helpful. This does not mean

1. *Tehillim*, 147:3
2. *Devarim*, 28:9
3. *Shabbos*, 133b
4. *Ohd Yosef Chai*, Parshas Tzav, 31–32

that a person should not address their mistakes. The question is how.

Regarding this, Rabbi Dessler taught that teshuva[5] and personal elevation are two sides of the same coin. Teshuva is about lifting oneself above darkness, to a place of light. It is about reaching a higher place and experiencing renewal.[6] If one's self-critique accomplishes this, then it is an integral part of teshuva. If it only brings one down, then it has nothing to do with teshuva.

Reflection

What are some examples of being compassionate to others?

How can I exercise compassion toward myself?

What are some things I can do to be a more compassionate person?

---

5. This is usually translated as *repentance*, but more accurately, it is the process of repairing our relationship with the divine.
6. *Michtav MeEliyahu*, 5, pp. 240–241

SHEPHERDS

Abraham, Isaac, and Jacob were all shepherds. So were Moses and David. When we look at their lives, we see men of exceptional ability. Could they not have found a better job than taking care of animals?

They probably could have. But it would not have given them what they were looking for. Taking care of the needs of animals, by day and by night, brings a person to humility. A humble person, being less absorbed with their own needs and wants, has more room to feel for someone else. This is what these shepherds were after.

These giants of character were not born with their excellence already realized. They engaged in a rigorous training program of compassion-development, through caring for their flocks. For years, they led their charges with patience and gentleness, sensitizing themselves to the needs of each. By developing such an exquisite feeling for animals, their levels of compassion for people became that much greater.[1]

It was not the intellectual prowess of these individuals, but rather, their compassion, which was responsible for their rise to leadership. We see this in the case of Moses. He was watching his father-in-law's flock in the wilderness. A goat ran away and he chased after it. The goat ran until it reached a pool of water, where it stopped to drink. When Moses caught up to it, he said, "I did not know that you were running because you were thirsty. Now, you must be tired. He lifted the goat onto his shoulder and walked it back to the herd. G-d said, "You have such compassion to treat animals in this way, so too, you shall be the shepherd of my flock, the children of Israel."[2]

---

1. *Chochma V'Mussar*, vol. 1, chap. 1
2. *Shemos Rabbah*, Parsha Beis

We find a similar story with King David. When he was a shepherd, he would prevent the older sheep from taking the food of the younger ones. He would first take out the smaller animals to eat from the softer grass. Afterward, he would take out the older sheep who would feed on the medium grass. And finally, he would take out the strongest sheep which would eat from the toughest grass. G-d said, "The one who knows how to take care of sheep, each according to its strength, let him come and be the shepherd of My nation."[3]

Developing excellence of character requires two vital steps: The first step is to clarify where we want to get to. The second step is to choose a path, humble as it may be, which will get us there. Without these two steps, our ability to develop ourselves does not have much traction.

Reflection

Where do I want to get to?

_____

_____

_____

_____

What is my plan to get there?

_____

_____

_____

_____

3. Ibid.

THE LOVE OF GIVING

Aristotle pondered the following question: "Why is the love of the giver for the receiver, greater than the love of the receiver for the giver?"[1] He concluded that it is because the pleasure of giving is much greater than that of receiving. Although this is a true observation, there is a much deeper truth to be told.

The Kabbalists taught that G-d is the ultimate goodness. The nature of that which is good is to bestow good.[2] Toward this end, G-d created an entire world in order to allow for giving,[3] because if there is no receiver, then there is no giver.

Since the primary force upon which the world was built was giving, it follows that man, who is created "in the image of G-d," should experience the greatest pleasure when engaged in giving. Receiving only serves a purpose, in that it allows for giving, but not as an end in itself. This is manifested in the relatively lesser feelings of joy experienced when one finds oneself on the receiving end, as compared to being on the giving end.[4]

Giving and receiving is more than a question of who is giving to whom. It is a question of focus. Sometimes people may give, but their aim in giving is some personal benefit they hope to achieve. The physical act may look like giving, but it is only a means to receiving.

At the same time, we are sometimes on the receiving end and neither need to be, nor want to be. However, realizing that the giver may be

1. *Daas Torah*, Shmini, p. 59
2. This is referring to Hashem's will and not Hashem Himself, Who is beyond any limit and therefore beyond any description.
3. Ramchal, *Daas Tevunos*, 18
4. *Daas Torah*, Shmini, p. 59

insulted or embarrassed if we refuse, we accept what they want to give. The receiver is giving something by taking on a role they do not want, for the sake of the other's feelings. This would qualify as giving, despite the fact that on a physical level, they are receiving.

There is a basic paradigm, which separates givers and takers. Givers perceive themselves as being in this world to contribute to a bigger picture. Takers see themselves as the bigger picture.

To illustrate, imagine entering a wedding hall. The tables are beautifully set and the food has been meticulously prepared. We are here because we were invited. It would be ridiculous to conclude that everything we see before us is about us. There is the inviter and there are the invited.

And yet, it is possible to come into this world and walk around with an attitude that whatever we see exists for us. It is possible to forget that everything was set up before we arrived by someone else. He is the Host and we are the guests.

Givers express the realization that they are guests in G-d's world by honoring their Host. They live to further His desire that the world be a place for giving. It should come as no surprise, therefore, that givers generally experience greater happiness and satisfaction in life. This is because they are living in a way which is true to who they are, and where they are.

Reflection

What are some examples of me being a giver?

_____

_____

_____

_____

What are some examples of me being a receiver?

_____

_____

_____

_____

How do I see my role in the world?

_____

_____

_____

_____

What are some things I can do to be more of a giver?

_____

_____

_____

_____

INDEPENDENT ACTION

One of the traits that defines a leader is the ability to act independently. One of the traits that defines a follower is the tendency to follow the lead set by others. Rabbi Nosson asked: For what reason were the Princes of the Tribes the first ones to contribute by the dedication of the altar in the tabernacle, whereas by the construction of the tabernacle itself, they were not?

He explained: In the case of the building of the tabernacle, the Princes said, "Let the people donate whatever they will, and whatever is missing, we will complete." Once they saw that the people gave everything that was necessary, they said, "What is left for us to do?" And they brought the stones for the breastplate of the High Priest. Since they had been lazy initially, a letter is left out of the spelling of the word "princes" when they are mentioned by the work of the tabernacle.[1]

The lack of a letter in the spelling of "princes" here is symbolic of a lacking in them. What was the lacking? They said that whatever the people do not bring (for the tabernacle), they will cover. That sounds pretty generous.

The Princes were the leaders of the Jewish people. For them to base what they would do upon the actions of others represents a distinct lack of leadership. They chose to react to what others would do instead of choosing what is appropriate for them do. They were reactive instead of proactive.

In an awkward situation, we may have noticed how people look around and see what everyone else is doing, and more or less react to that? How much of our lives is lived in reaction to something someone else said, or did, or did not do?

1. Rashi, Parshas Vayakhel

What this means is that on some level, we have abdicated our life path to someone else, and are living out a script written by someone else. This is the opposite of choosing who and what we want to be, and living according to that standard. Such behavior is like being a slave of many masters, bound to follow the whims of those around us.

Being a free person means having the ability to step outside oneself and decide how to respond to the situation presented. It means having the ability to respond to stimuli according to thought-out values, instead of just reacting. It means being able to access more of who we really are and want to be, and living from there.

The missing letter from the word "Princes" was the Hebrew letter "yud." The letter "yud" symbolizes the faculty of thought.[2] It is very revealing that this was the letter that was left out of their name. On some level, there was an absence of the type of thought which is expected from leaders of the Jewish nation.

Reflection

What are some examples of when I have followed the lead of others?

_____

_____

What are some examples of when I have followed my own path?

_____

_____

How often am I in the role of a leader and how often am I in the role of a follower?

_____

_____

What is my experience of each?

_____

_____

2. *Shaarei Orah*, "Chochma"

INSIDE OUT

It is easy to fall into the trap of living someone else's life. Our environment acts on us constantly and the door of reactivity beckons to us to enter. Keeping balance and leaning on the staff of reflection to steady ourselves can take the strength of a Samson.

Our culture makes its demands. Be normal and fit in. Our family has their demands. We would not want to embarrass or disappoint them, of course. And the air we breathe teems with a multitude of messages pulling us in different directions.

Our breath quickens and we pump our legs, breaking into a sprint. Time is limited and we have to get there. But where are we running?

Phrases like "I could hardly breathe" or "I didn't have time to catch my breath" are part of our daily vernacular. We are paying a price – our life's breath. But what are we getting for it?

It is interesting that we can pay so much and fail to ask this question.

There are two paths before us. One is outside-in and the other is inside-out. The outer world makes its move and we can either react or respond.

Reacting means that what we do is largely determined by factors outside ourselves, like a puppet whose strings are being pulled from behind the scenes. To respond means that the force behind our action is a product of personal thought and conviction. It is an informed reply mirroring the deeper waters of reflection we have cultivated within ourselves.

There is an inner well from which we can draw resourcefulness. It is dug in those quiet moments when we allow ourselves to contemplate who we are and what we are doing here. By investing time in great questions like these, and others like, "What did the giants of spirit who walked the Earth before me do?" and "What was special about them that brought them close to G-d?"[1] we can bridge the gap between who we can be and who we are now.

Reflection

What are some examples of the values I cherish?

_____

_____

_____

_____

How do I apply these values in my life?

_____

_____

_____

_____

How much time do I invest daily in self-reflection?

_____

_____

_____

_____

Who am I?

_____

_____

_____

_____

1. Ramchal, *Derech Eitz Chaim*

KEEPING IT FRESH

In Satmar, as in many yeshivos, it was the custom to put on a humorous play on the holiday of Purim. Oftentimes, the yeshiva students would imitate the teachers of the yeshiva in jest. One year a young man decided to imitate the Satmar Rebbe's Rosh Hashana davening (prayers). The young man was brilliant. He bowed back and forth, gesticulating, and sounding just like the Rebbe. The Rebbe, looking on, started to cry. The young man, taken aback at the Rebbe's reaction, naturally stopped. But the Rebbe encouraged him to keep on with his act. And as the young man continued mimicking the Rebbe, the Rebbe cried more and more. The scene was quite bizarre.

Afterward, someone mustered the courage to ask the Rebbe what that was all about. The Rebbe explained that as he saw the young man imitate him so well, he couldn't help but think to himself that perhaps in all his devotions, he was just imitating what he had done the previous year. And the more he thought about it, the more this worry pierced his heart.

It is so easy to fall into the pattern of living life as a rerun. The Prophet Isaiah poignantly expressed this tendency: "... When this nation approaches Me (G-d), they honor Me with their mouths and their lips, but their hearts are far from Me. Their fear of me is akin to the service of those who perform by rote."[1] G-d was calling out to the nation – Open your hearts! When you pray, make it mean something!

Prayer devoid of thought is like a body without a soul.[2] If we want our words to reach the heavens, we need to invest them with the power to get there. That power comes from our intent. When we think about

1. *Isaiah,* 29:13
2. *Shenei Luchos HaBris,* Maseches Tamid

Whom we are standing before, and what we are saying, our words become invested with a superior quality. They are alive.

Being alive and performing acts which are filled with vitality requires thought. Without investing what we say and what we do with intent, the most meaningful acts can become meaningless, or worse. The divine becomes mundane. And we are left feeling disconnected, because we are.

So how do we keep it fresh?

Be mindful. Think about what we are doing and why are we doing it. Think about who we are and what we are here for.[3] Thinking about big questions gives us the focus which keeps us alive.

Reflection

Which parts of my life feel like a rerun when I do them?

_____

_____

_____

_____

How much intent do I invest in my actions?

_____

_____

_____

_____

Which parts of my life feel more alive?

_____

_____

_____

_____

What are some things I can do to revitalize the parts which feel less alive?

_____

_____

_____

_____

3. Ramchal, *Derech Eitz Chaim*

ACTION

Action changes us. The Jewish people, leaving Egypt, experienced the highest levels of revelation. But they did not earn it, so it did not last. It was not a product of their actions, so it did not become part of them.

Only after climbing level after level for forty-nine days, through the sweat of their brows, were the Jews ready to receive revelation and hold onto it. That which they had experienced leaving Egypt and lost, they received at Sinai and kept.

Every year on the first night of Passover, this pattern repeats itself. All the supernal lights shine upon Israel. But it has the quality of a handout and not something earned. It is elevating, but does not stick without a follow-up.[1]

G-d commands us to follow up: "Count for yourselves – for your benefit, for your good." On each day of the sefirah (counting – the forty-nine days we count between the time of leaving Egypt and the receiving of the Torah), there is another facet of spirituality made available to us. G-d instructs us: Work on yourselves and integrate this growth! This is the meaning behind the different kabbalistic attributes which correspond to the different days of the counting.[2] Each is representative of another facet of character growth.

From Passover until the holiday of Shavuos, we count seven days a week for seven weeks. Seven represents a totality. Existence is sevenfold: Up, down, right, left, forward, backward, and then an inner point of unity from which all the other directions branch forth.[3]

---

1. *B'nei Yissachar*, Sivan, 1
2. Found in the kabbalistic tefillah following the counting of the Omer.
3. Maharal, *Gevuros Hashem*, chap. 46

All of our days derive their life force from this inner point of unity. It is a point of holiness, which lies at the core of all existence. Our work is to see and reveal this inner energy even in the mundane, and reconnect it to its source.[4]

The way we do this is by acting on the world, using physicality as an agent of revelation. The Torah is an instruction book of how to do this. By performing the different commandments of the Torah, we are taking physical constructs and through them, expressing an inner divinity.

This is what it means to be an Adam, a human being. The name Adam means one who was taken from the adama, the earth (*adama* is the Hebrew word for "earth"). Earth represents a potential, which needs work to bring forth its fruit. So too man, through his actions, has the power to bring forth his fruit, his inner abundance.

Reflection

What kind of fruit am I producing?

_____

_____

_____

What type and amount of action would produce better fruit?

_____

_____

_____

Which actions do I feel particularly connected to?

_____

_____

_____

What can I do to develop excellence in this area?

_____

_____

_____

4. *Sfas Emes*, Likkutim, Parshas Eikev

CONCLUSION

The wisdom of self-knowledge is one of the most difficult and most rewarding to acquire. An ongoing effort is required to penetrate our façade, and see beneath the masks we show to the world, and to ourselves. Only by listening carefully to our hearts and cultivating sensitivity to what is there will we come to know our inner depths.

As we become better listeners, an awareness of cause and effect, of our successes as well as our failures, expands within. With this awareness comes the realization that our actions and our lives are our responsibility alone. Our goal is to make the most of both of them, utilizing our self-understanding. True success in life is always from the inside out.

This is what Akavia ben Mahallelel taught his son, as his son was close to death:

"Father, speak on my behalf to your friends [that they should help me in the next world]," the son asked his father.

"I'm not going to," his father responded.

"Perhaps, you have found some fault in me?" his son asked.

"No. Your actions will bring you close, and your actions will distance you,"[1] his father replied.

No recommendations can compensate for what we are not. Our actions alone draw us close, or keep us away from connecting to the Source of all life. When we stop looking outward to succeed, and shift our focus within, we have taken the most crucial step toward becoming our greatest selves.

---

1. *Mishnayos Eduyos*, 5:7